DESIGNS
WE LIVE BY

Edited by
Helga Loeb, Phil Slight
and Nick Stanley

NATIONAL SOCIETY FOR EDUCATION IN ART & DESIGN

Acknowledgements

We gratefully acknowledge all those who have helped develop the Ethnographic Resources for Art Education project. The following people worked directly for the project: Pauline Amphlett, Margaret Beckford, Yvonne Brierley, Heather Brown, Sue Burke, Julie Davies, Joan Gibbons, Kathryn Hemmings, Patrick Hunt, Gillian King, Simon Lilly, Maureen McElleran, Ian McFadyan, Sally Moore, Alex Rammage, Davinda Sandhu, Barbara Scanes, Michele Scully, Wade Turner, Roy Upson, David Wellings.

We would also like to thank Rashida Noor-mohammed who helped launch ERAE and Allan Leary, chair of the Changing Traditions Teachers Group and all its members who worked in developing curriculum materials; the Editors of Ceramic Review for permission to reproduce part of Jonathan Slye's article in Ceramic Review No. 48; The Centre of West African Studies, Birmingham University, for permission to reproduce a Nupe pot from the Danford Collection; Birmingham Museums and Art Gallery for permission to reproduce textile designs from the Applied Arts Collection, and a gold coin from the Archeology and Ethnography Collection.

We acknowledge the continual support of museums and curators, particularly at Birmingham Museum, British Museum (especially the Museum of Mankind), National Museum of Ireland, Royal Museum of Scotland, Pitt Rivers Museum, Victoria and Albert Museum. We thank all the specialists who advised us throughout the project. Finally we owe thanks to our colleagues in the Department of Art and the Research Committee of Birmingham Institute of Art & Design, University of Central England.

Helga Loeb, Phil Slight, Nick Stanley

CONTENTS

Preface

This book grows from a series of linked research and curriculum development publications from *Ethnographic Resources for Art Education (ERAE)*. The intention of this work is to engage in the kind of research which an interested teacher of art, craft and design could expect to undertake, given sufficient time. We hope that the work done by ourselves and our researchers will appeal directly to teachers and students and convince them that it is possible to approach unfamiliar cultures from modest beginnings. We have had the advantage of being able to employ a number of graduate researchers and designers, and to have access to specialist advice in each field we have tackled. The four popular topics dealt with in this book are selected from the following complete list of ERAE publications:

Ashanti and Hausa Pottery
Pottery from Peru
Pottery from Pakistan
Dyed and Printed Textiles (Java, Holland and West Africa)
The Art of Play
Celtic Art and Design
Projects and Prospects (conference proceedings)
The Visual Arts and Multicultural Education
Changing Traditions I (exhibition catalogue)
Changing Traditions II (conference proceedings)

Studies by individual teachers published by ERAE:

Mary Richards: Peruvian Weaving
Lawrie Thorne: The Mexican Tree of Life
Chris Toye: Bilas, Body Decoration in New Guinea

All of these, except **The Visual Arts and Multicultural Education** (available from London University School of Oriental Studies, Extramural Division Publications) are available via Educational Research Information Centre (ERIC) on CD-ROM.

As each topic was researched, interesting cross references became apparent as, for example, in decorative patterns on Hausa dwellings and elements of Islamic and Celtic calligraphy. These open up possibilities for studying design links between different but related cultures. In this book we have respected the style of the four original texts. Each has a particular flavour and the studies in this book reflect this individuality. We have tried, however, to demonstrate the underlying thematic unity of the project as a whole. The introduction, which follows, deals with the challenge of making cross-cultural comparisons.

1. INTRODUCTION

Designs We Live By

Understanding perspectives other than our own is a vital necessity in a rapidly changing world. This is as true in the field of art and design as in any other discipline. As more and more people come to reassert cultural identity, the ability to interpret and engage with each other becomes the more vital. As ethnic identity reasserts itself it is tempting to use multicultural approaches as a quick solution to the apparent problems. Cross-cultural study, this book argues, must offer depth and respect for the contents of the culture under study. Whilst the mosaic of cultures may initially seem bewilderingly complex, yet, if we adopt specific methods of investigation we may come to see this diversity as a richness rather than a source of disquiet.

A decisive factor may be whether the learning about other cultures is presented in a manner that celebrates diversity and thus makes overt appeal to values which support understanding and harmony in a pluralist society.

In this sense we believe that ethnographically based visual resource information together, perhaps, with narrative material can be useful to teachers and pupils in all areas, leaving them free to connect the images and ideas drawn from other cultures with their own interests and experience.

The use of wider cultural reference is frequently adopted with enthusiasm in primary education, but less in secondary. This may be partly because integrated cross-discipline work is more commonly used in the primary curriculum. Projects involving personal exploration of the natural world by young people realistically involve natural sciences, writing, drawing and painting, and even photography and computer imaging. Such relaxed boundary crossing is seldom as easily accomplished at secondary level. But many GCSE syllabuses permit and encourage a broadly based approach to art and design. The National Curriculum also increases the attractiveness of combined approaches to specific themes for many disciplines. The limited time allocated to individual foundation subjects makes the pooling of time and effort by subject specialisms worth the extra effort.

A Range of Design Studies

What this publication offers, in addition to some examples of a multicultural approach to art and design education, is a range of design studies which explore the cultural matrix from which the designs emanate. Each study expresses a distinctive set of perspectives that may challenge the student preparing for GCSE, or A level art and design. The projects have implications for other subject areas, particularly craft, design technology, communication and media studies, cultural studies, and comparative philosophy and religion. The most striking feature of these design studies is the way in which they enter and change accepted notions of design. Truly they can be said to become part of the designs we live by.

Wisdom is not received, it is acquired. In each person's mind the fundamental concepts of the world have to be reconstructed. This is a tenet of educational theory, but it has not yet received much attention in art and design education. Construction - yes; it fills and spills over from art and design classrooms everywhere, but fundamental concepts - no. Specialist art teachers might claim that art represents a special form of 'knowing', but, immersed in the making of images and objects, they are seldom able to articulate how such understanding comes about. Yet, in the process of concept formation the very nature of art offers the opportunity to make visible and understood fugitive and ephemeral ideas which come and, too often, go in the flux of teaching and learning. Other disciplines call on visualization as an aid, but it is primarily a technique used in the service of another objective. In art, craft and design the peculiarly concentrated understanding derived from the linked acts of seeing and giving form is central.

Learning to Think

We owe to J. S. Bruner a model of how experience comes to be represented in the mind: thought is rooted in physical activity, represented in imagery, and distilled by abstraction in symbolic form. To deal in this sequence with all the concepts that have to be grasped by the pupil would surely lack both the economy and power that Bruner requires of instruction; but it is appropriate for any educator to consider what concepts result from any particular area of study. Art education is in a particularly favourable position to contribute to the development of mature judgement, since its contents and procedures encompass Bruner's three modes of representation quite naturally. Art teachers have a responsibility, therefore, for helping their pupils to use iconic representation as a component of symbolic thought – to link making to meaning.

In the case of our present concerns, sometimes the concept to be learned will be specifically located within art, craft or design: for example, techniques of shaping and firing examined in the context of different geographical and economic settings. At other times attention may be given to a concept of universal significance expressed in visual form, as demonstrated by Feldman in four sculptures of pregnant women – by Degas (c. 1896-1911), Epstein (1931), Picasso (1950), and a Fertility Fetish from the lower Congo. (1) The understanding of the pupil in this instance would refer to pregnancy as life experience, the images as representations of that experience and the abstraction of certain salient ideas – weight, distortion of shape, the woman's response to her condition. Comparison of the sculptures **is** possible in relation to an **identified** concept, and as it happens, the Fetish seems to possess the greatest expressive power. The point to stress is that the judgements involved are not global, about cultures, but specific. The argument relies on the organisation of evidence, and that is what education is about – not a branch of special education called 'multicultural', but education as such.

What concepts?

What concepts should a multicultural approach to art education promote? The following suggestions may indicate some criteria by which teachers could judge how certain areas of the syllabus could be brought into sharper focus, maybe by expansion, but primarily by a change in emphasis and the use of reference material drawn from many cultures.

1   The interaction of environmental needs and resources, techniques and cultural forms.

2   The discovery of the pupil's own creativity and competence, as a basis for acknowledging and valuing the creativity and competence of others. (An example from our **Playthings as Art Objects** (2) pack might be the act of making and playing a sound-producing object which would in turn set a standard for the appreciation of one of the traditional objects described in the text.)

3   Gaining experience of the characteristics of materials, and sensitivity to their properties and qualities, e.g. hardness, brittleness, pliability, and their suitability for carving, moulding, hardening by fire.

4   The characteristics of human activity. Artists and craftworkers may be seen in the context of **3** (above) as having certain qualities and predispositions, and these too, become media of artistic expression. An example of this is the human propensity to create symbolic transitional forms, as in imaginative play which provides a bridge between the here and now and some other realm of the spirit or imagination.

5   The qualities of objects in terms of aesthetic content, function and craftwork seen as response to the problems posed by the needs of a society, or the perceptions of individuals. The exotic aspects of certain artefacts from strange cultures are therefore tempered by identification of problems and solutions. Seen in this light the object becomes a means of communication.

Nothing said so far falls outside the range of the normal art/craft/design curriculum, and could perhaps be regarded as comparative art education. In this sense a reference to Comparative Religion might prove useful, in providing a more familiar parallel. Children are nurtured in the religion of their family by induction to its customs, practice and belief – as they are encouraged to make art in the schools of their community. To learn **about** religions, as systems by which human beings order their lives, is to adopt a wider perspective. It is to attempt to interpret and understand the customs and practices of others, without necessarily adopting them as one's own; hence the parallel with multicultural reference in art education.

Three Key Ideas

Three key ideas in an ethnographic approach to art education would, however, introduce a change of emphasis. The first is to use ethnographic information to emphasize **common needs, common problems and a comparison of solutions.** For example, an important concept in many societies is that of Divine Kingship. A fascinating area of study opens up when we consider how this concept has been variously interpreted and represented - from the monolithic heads and half-length figures of Easter Island, to the faces on the towers of Angkor, compared with earlier Egyptian royal statues and the Great Sphinx, and perhaps with European painting and sculpture.

The second key concept is the acceptance, indeed **celebration of diversity.** This may be especially well learned in a field where there are no 'correct' answers; in art diversity is the essence of the subject matter itself.

A third essential objective must surely be to strengthen an understanding of how **cultural influences spread and interact.** Most people learn something at school about trade routes, or the migration of peoples in search of security, space, glory, adventure or wealth, as the case may be. In the arts and crafts such information can become personally significant when changes in techniques are experienced by means of actual, physical involvement in processes and materials, leading to changes in style being recognized as part of a whole constellation of cultural influences. The examples of the characteristic blue and white colour scheme which we in the West associate with Chinese porcelains is a case where such influences may be acknowledged through attention to process. The colour is the result of new techniques introduced to China during the Mongol conquest, and evolved under their rule by a marriage of Chinese and Iranian processes and materials.

'China provides the porcelain, ... Iran the cobalt oxide medium used for decorating Near Eastern earthenware. This was the most easily controllable medium for underglaze decorations, and was at first used in China for motifs of an Iranian cast on porcelain vessels fashioned like the metal work of the Mongols. During the Ming period the colour-scheme persisted, but all traces of foreign influence were expunged from the designs and Ming blue-white porcelain is as purely Chinese in decoration as in form.' (4)

Future Developments

In conclusion, it might be useful to consider future developments. As we have seen, curriculum content can range across cultures in what might become a stimulating and productive extension of current practice. The task now is to provide examples and resources which are clearly presented in terms of artistic and **social** diversity. Of almost equal priority is the need to develop a style of communication which ensures a wide dissemination of such materials. Another important aspect is to monitor development and use of materials in classrooms. Packs of ethnographic resources act as points of departure for a wide variety of lessons. Close scrutiny is needed into how they are used, and with what results. In this sensitive area the approach can be innovative, exciting and celebratory. Or, mishandled, albeit with good intentions, it may lead to defensive attitudes towards 'multicultural' content. We are convinced, therefore, that our endeavours must justify themselves as beneficial practice in general arts education, and not as special pleading. More information is needed about how teachers adapt the materials to their particular needs; their contact with other subject specialists - we know already that they have been found useful in Social Studies and Home Economics, where they have engendered extra-curricular activities and interests. All such initiatives will stand in some relation to class composition, and teacher and pupil attitudes and perceptions.

Accepting Limitations

When all has been said and done, we shall have to accept the limitations on complete multicultural understanding. Honour and Fleming put it well:

'The arts of Africa, like some of those of Oceania, and the American North-West, lose their all-important fourth dimension when uprooted and taken out of their ritual contexts - just as people living in urbanized and industrialized societies tend to lose their sixth sense.' (5)

We believe that responding to art objects from other cultures through imaginative construction and personal interpretation begins to restore to them that fourth dimension which they lack as museum objects.

The claims for a multicultural approach to art education are modest: merely to widen the cultural reference of the curriculum. Within the comparing, contrasting and valuing thus engendered, there should emerge a stronger sense of their own identity for all participants in the process: black or white, all seeing themselves as part of a bigger picture.

What Traditions, What Changes?

In using ethnographic reference it would be foolish to ignore the problems of attempting to cross traditional barriers and enter someone else's territory with all its undeclared meanings and assumptions. It is precisely because the resource materials try to locate objects in an authentic context that they should encourage sensitivity in avoiding spurious contrasts and misleading comparison. No doubt both kinds of mistake, and others, will be made on occasions. The bedrock of common ground between all cultures is the cycle of human life experiences. There are enough artefacts which may be related to this pattern in the context of exploring techniques and identifying common problems.

If one were to imagine oneself, for a moment, as a pupil in, for example, a lesson on Islamic patterns, what would it take to consider that one had 'done' it, and that one knew all about it? It seems, on the contrary, that a good lesson would leave a sense of passing acquaintance or perhaps an aroused interest, to be resuscitated on a future occasion.

Such interest, once engaged, is bound to lead to at least this recognition: that all traditions, except in the most isolated communities, are subject to change. Even young children can understand the parameters of their lessons, and their sharp observation makes its own connections with the world outside and through the media. One group of Juniors noted that though they had been learning about traditional Japanese customs and objects, their activities were being recorded on modern Japanese video equipment. The implication for this project is that while traditional art forms demonstrate most tellingly the connection between the artefact and the physical and cultural environment from which it originates, the objects are always plucked out for inspection at a particular point in time. Preserved in museum show-cases they are specimens; studied, connected with people, and re-interpreted, they acquire new life. A tradition has changed, or even disappeared, but some of its qualities are translated into a new context. All pupils in a plural society are part of that new context.

Above: House of Mallam dan Wawu, Kano, Nigeria. Decorated by Mallam Inuwa dan Umaru, c. 1938.

Changes in the curriculum impose new disciplines, especially on the teacher. A degree of care is needed in tempering the search for 'multicultural activities' with informed and sensitive attitudes towards materials drawn from very different ways of life, and from people whose view of the world may not be easily apprehended. The radical change, therefore, is in the deliberate insertion of humanistic components into the art curriculum.

It will not be easily achieved, but looking at the vigour and variety of the work produced by many different schools one may begin to see it as a step towards underpinning relationships in a multicultural society. Pupils are often as quick to see cross-cultural potential in their design projects as their teachers. For example, in one lesson a sixth form student drew on her personal knowledge of Indian and British folklore in order to compare them with the symbolism of motifs appearing on Yoruba Adire cloth.

The four studies that follow take up the themes addressed in this introduction. Each study develops a different aspect of the design process. The difference relates not only to historical eras but to the very way in which design as an activity figures in Islamic, African, Celtic and Japanese culture, history, the technical development of media and aesthetic sensibility.

Notes:

1   E. B. Feldman: *Varieties of Visual Experience,* Harry N. Abrahams Inc., New York, p.660

2   *Ethnographic Resources for Art Education; Playthings as Art Objects.* Roy Upson, et al: 'Sound-Making Objects', 1983.

3   H. Honour and J. Fleming: *A World History of Art,* Macmillan, U.K., 1982, p.549

4   Ibid., p.415

5   Ibid., p.416

2. Islamic Design

2. ISLAMIC PATTERN

Islamic design employs principles of construction that develop into an abstract system of endlessly repeating and changing motifs. The designs can be found not only in tile work and architecture but also in woven textiles.

Endlessness may be suggested in two ways by a work of art: either by an all-over field of colour, or by a grid with a sufficient number of repetitions. In Islamic pattern the parts of a design are horizontally, vertically and diagonally repeated, reflected and rotated; however, though it is absolutely regular, the system does not result in a simple prediction or confirmation in reading a pattern, but rather creates a feeling of endless permutation as a number of different patterns overlap and interlock.

Each carpet and tile work is discrete and may be understood conceptually, yet the visual experience of the pattern is dynamic, multiform, and ungraspable. This is the essence of Islamic design: the unified, systematic pattern contains diverse reading, and a few formal principles of design give rise to a continual fluctuation in perception and consequently create a sensation of limitless expansion. In Islam pattern of this kind trancends the aesthetic experience and becomes, in E.H.Gombrich's phrase, 'a visual metaphor of value'. The unifying

system, containing diversity, becomes expressive of the balance of forces which are spriritual: part/whole, stability/dynamism, completeness/endlessness. In this way, quite an abstract pattern may be interpreted as paradigmatic of moral and spiritual value, quite apart from the history of its use in mosque and private prayer carpet. This approach is demonstrated by the mystical system of the Sufis; although many Orthodox Muslims think that Sufi philosophy is too influenced by Western thought, it does show how pattern in Islam may be treated as a visual metaphoric language, a diagrammatic language which appeals to the intellect. There is no pictorial iconography in Islam comparable to that found in Christian art, despite the frequent use of certain symbols and figurative devices; but pattern conveys religious feeling through formal order – balance as the basic principle of harmonious life, the human order reflecting the Divine order. Sura LV of the Koran says:

'He hath created man
He hath taught him power of expression
The sun and the moon are made punctual...
And the sky he hath uplifted;
And he hath set the balance
That ye exceed not the balance
But observe it strictly, or fall short thereof'.

Above: A tile panel above an outer courtyard window, Fatin Mosque, Istanbul, 1470

12

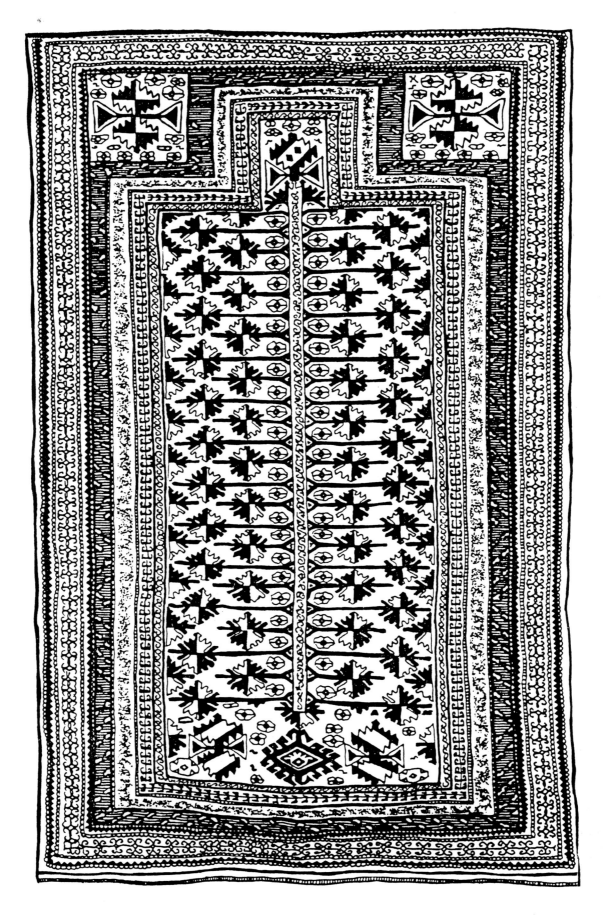

Above: A Baluchi Tree of Life prayer rug with Baluchi tribal guls in the spandrels of the geometric mihrab. The gul is a sign of tribal identity, and part of this Baluchi gul is used for the flowers on the tree's branches, so that the tree stands for the tribal group with the branches representing its generations. This conceptual design is the origin of the 'family tree' diagram used in the western world. Like the multiple prayer carpet, in the context of the mihrab, it relates the social group to the great family of Muslims.

This section concentrates specifically on the Islamic carpet and the way in which it relates to religious belief and practice. The techniques of manufacture are described and the most complex and beautiful of these carpets, the court carpets, are shown as the high point of artistic achievement. The changes in production brought about by mechanised production are also considered.

The Mihrab

Rugs and carpets are commodities throughout the Islamic world, with an important and understood place in commerce and trade. At the same time, they possess a magic and mystery bound up with the history of nomadic life, the secrets of the dyer's art, and with the use of the carpet in meditation. More specifically, certain rugs called **mihrabs** are used in the act of prayer, and this religious significance, by association, lends all carpets a precious quality. The mihrab is the arch-shaped prayer niche in the mosque which indicates the direction of the **Kaaba**, the sacred shrine in Mecca, the Holy City. It is this arched shape which gives the prayer carpet its essential, characteristic design, and its name. Prayer carpets are used in the **Salat**, or Daily Prayer, which is one of the five religious duties of the Muslim faith. The Salat requires a Muslim to pray five times a day with his or her face turned towards Mecca; there the Kaaba is situated in a cloistered courtyard in the centre of the Great Mosque. The Kaaba is fifty feet high and draped in black silk, and it contains a black meteoric stone which Islam teaches was given to Abraham by Allah. The Kaaba is of ancient origin and was a holy place before Mohammed preached Islam. Once, when the Kaaba had been damaged by heavy rains and the stone dislodged from its niche, the various clans of the Quraysh tribe which ruled Mecca could not agree upon who should replace the stone. They asked the first man to enter the temple courtyard to choose. This man was Mohammed, and he solved the problem by placing the stone in the centre of his own robe so that all the clan leaders could hold the cloth together and raise the stone to its niche. This story shows how before the foundation of the Islamic faith, Mohammed had been able to unite people in a common religious purpose: when Muslims kneel in prayer today, they too are bound together by a shared devotion.

The mihrab arch of the prayer carpet may be pointed, or rectangular, or curved, depending upon the preferred form and the method of weaving employed: the simplest horizontal loom most easily lends itself to the creation of straight-lined, stepped, rectangular arches. Whatever the design, the function is the same: unrolled so that it points, like the Mihrab niche in the mosque, towards Mecca. The prayer carpet symbolically relates the man or woman or child at prayer to the spiritual and

geographical heart of Islam. Wherever they may be, the Faithful turn towards the place which is the centre of their religion, and the prayer carpet enables those who are unable to visit a mosque to feel properly directed in the Salat. Communal prayer carpets contain several mihrabs, visually and practically embodying the idea of prayer as a shared experience. Mohammed himself said that prayer in a mosque is better than prayer in private, and the multiple prayer arch design – known as the **Saph** design – symbolizes the social value of prayer: although one may pray alone, anywhere, group prayer in a particular place brings people together in

Above: A Muslim at prayer before the mihrab niche in a mosque: he kneels upon a carpet which reflects this essential shape. The architectural mihrab shown here was once used by the Prophet Mohammed himself for his daily prayers.

14

a feeling of kinship which emphasises social responsibility. Some Saph carpets are family prayer rugs, and here the individual family group becomes a symbol of the great family of Muslims.

Mohammed himself did not know the prayer carpet, and the Koran does not include the command to say your prayer kneeling on one, but later commentaries on the Koran include instructions to kneel on something clean, and heavy enough not to be blown away by the wind when praying. Although we cannot be sure when the prayer carpet was invented, we do know from Persian minature paintings that they existed by the 15th century, and eventually became widespread, a profound image of the call to prayer. Islam might be called the religion of prayer since no other faith places such emphasis upon regular and frequent prayer. The word 'mosque' itself means 'place of kneeling', and from the minaret the **Muezzin** has for centuries called to the Faithful:

> 'Allahu akbar, Allahu akbar...
> God is most great, God is most great...
> There is no God but Allah,
> Mohammed is his messenger...
> Come to prayer, come to prayer...'

Above: Ghiordes mid-18th century knotted wool prayer carpet showing two pillars and a hanging oil lamp: the architectural space of the mosque is translated into a two-dimensional formal design.

Above: A mosque in Isfahan showing the mihrab and the minbar. Patterns in the mosque change with the light and sometimes disappear in shadow: a constantly changing, ungraspable visual experience.

15

Woven Architecture

Weaving is thread construction, a process which lends itself to the creation of artefacts which are light and portable and hard-wearing. Storage and travelling bags, camel saddlebags, grain sacks and spindle bags have all been important in the life of nomadic people. But like the carpet which has the practical function of keeping down dust in summer and providing warmth in winter, and the dividing curtain which provides privacy and insulation in the tent, these artefacts are given aesthetic and symbolic appeal too. Carpets and cushions are made for comfort: they are the furniture of nomadic tents, and their usefulness being bound up in human relaxation, it is easy to understand how they came to be patterned for visual pleasure. The patterning of utilitarian objects such as bags and sacks; and the camel blanket on which the rider's leg rests, is a way of recognising the importance of such objects in daily life. Other nomadic woven pieces have no utilitarian purpose and are patterned in order to celebrate a special occasion such as a wedding or to demonstrate pride in the possession of a particular animal or object. And, of course, the pattern expresses the culture and sensibility of the weaver. The camel's brightly patterned headstall, or the **Libad**, a camel and litter decoration made of multi-coloured patterned sections hung with tassels and ornamented with blue glass rings used on festive days and at tribal weddings – these works provide pleasure, express significance, and confer meaning. Weaving, which creates materials which are light, transportable, and perishable, would seem to be quite the opposite of the architecture of fixed buildings in its characteristics. But the two are related in process, history and function. Building

Below: Today many nomads have settled and the revenues from oil have brought new roads to the desert. Though trucks speed past the camel, nomadic life does continue and with it, two significant features of the nomadic ecology: light, easily transportable and hard-wearing fabrics, and the camel which carries the people and their belongings.

and weaving both create form by constructing with separate parts which are visible as structural units in the completed work; both are even older than pottery or metal work where the process fuses the material elements, rather than linking them together. Both building and weaving have provided people with shelter: one for a settled life, and one for a travelling life. Woven fabrics have satisfied a need for an effective shelter which would be quickly and easily assembled and dismantled, which could be rolled and folded to a reduced size, and which was light enough to be transportable.

Below: The tent of a sheik in the Nufud desert; the roof provides shade, walls are absent to allow air to circulate. The tent provides a meeting place where Bedouin extend hospitality: coffee and tea, lamb and pilaf, dates and camel's milk. To the Bedouin hospitality is a sacred duty.

Below: This trapping is used to decorate the head and neck of a camel at Turkoman bridal processions. It is a patchwork of flannel and cotton with embroidered motifs and feathers and buttons sewn on.

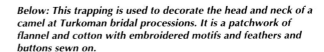

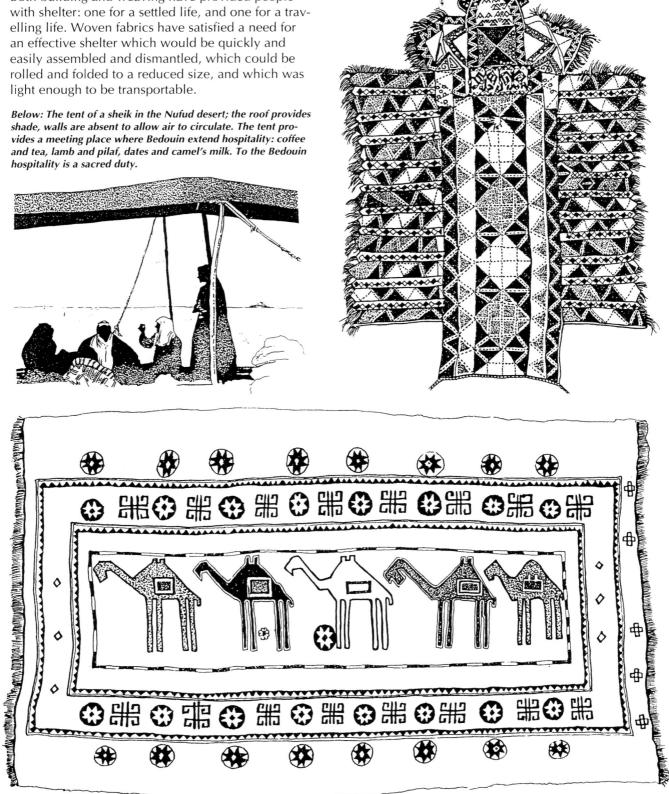

Above: Caucasian tribal rugs sometimes include stylized camel motifs in the central field. Mohammed himself worked as a guide on the camel caravans that carried frankincense and silk through Mecca to the north of Syria.

17

The Tent as a Flexible Home

Tents are still vital to the nomadic peoples of the world and these 'textile houses' allow people to travel in arid areas where no natural shelters, or materials for the construction of shelters, exist. Today in villages in Jordan, Lebanon, and Syria, strips of material are woven on vertical looms by male weavers for the walls and roofs of Bedouin tents: and the tent is called **Bayt al-sha'ar**, or 'house of hair'. The tent is a house which is flexible both in material and in design: the fabric from which its parts are made is pliable, and the arrangement of the tent walls may be varied according to circumstances. Since the walls are neither rigid nor supporting, they can be raised and tied back to ventilate the tent when it is hot. In cold weather another characteristic of the woven textiles becomes apparent: insulating quality, which helps to retain heat. Significantly, the parts of a Bedouin tent are called by names which refer back to the human body. The front corner poles are 'hands', the back corner poles 'legs', and the front of the tent 'the face' and the back of the tent 'the back of the head'. The tent is a habitation which is woven of insulating and pliable material; it is both a house and a third skin which protects the user from the weather, like the clothes we wear on our bodies which are our second skin. The **Abagah** of the Bedouin of North Arabia is a sleeveless cloak which envelops the body of the wearer, almost like a small tent. Weaving fabricates a counterpart to the animal hides which first clothed people, and was used for its ability to expand when wet and shed rainwater, to protect from the wind and provide shade. Today, when as travellers, we become 'temporary nomads' ourselves, we still use the tent as a travelling home. If the first shelters were wattle structures, woven from animal hides, bark and leaves, then this method of building, along with the development of basket weaving, gives rise to structural principles which were then utilised in weaving with yarn spun from animal hair. This is clear in the examples of twined weft patterns. The weaver uses two strands of weft thread at a time and with the fingers inserts one over and one under one, two or three warp threads to make diamonds, a technique which is essentially the same as that used in twined basketry. There is a balanced interplay in the weaving process between material constraints and the active forming on the part of the weaver: the Bedouin tent shows that physical constraints may largely determine the pattern of the woven walls. The walls and roof are too large to be woven on even a large vertical loom; consequently they are made up of woven strips of goat hair and wool cloth which are sewn together. The fitting together of different sections inevitably creates patterns and these are usually accentuated by cotton strips in the wool cloth. If this seems to be an *ad hoc* form of pattern dictated by practical consideration alone, then the collage process behind it was also used for the tent dividing curtain, and this has aesthetic and symbolic appeal. The curtain dividing the men's and women's sections of the tent separates the public and private domains as is customary in Islam. It is usually patterned and the 'good' side of

Below: Section of a tent dividing curtain made by the Bedouin of Jordan; woven strips are sewn together, patterned pieces alternating with plain weave. The horizontal rows and vertical rectangular sections create a structural grid.

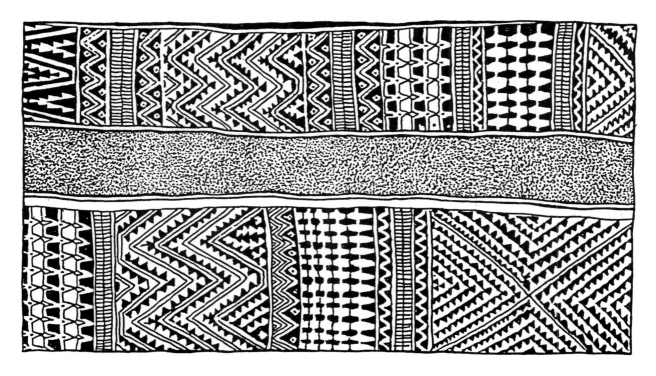

Above: The dividing curtain is hung so that its 'good' side faces into the men's section of the tent where guests are received and tribal business discussed: the patterned curtain plays a part in the ritual of hospitality.

the weave faces into the men's section where public entertainment and discussion of tribal business takes place. The pattern is the result of joining different woven pieces in horizontal bands and in vertical, rectangular sections. Patterned rugs and cushions are brought from storage in the women's section when guests arrive and are laid out in the men's section. In fact, before guests arrive there is very little to furnish the men's section, and the curtain will not be fully drawn. The extension of the curtain and the unrolling of rug and piling up of cushions are therefore seen to be acts of hospitality. In this context pattern does more than provide visual appeal: it functions actively in the ritual of honouring guests.

The relation of pattern and hospitality is shown by those dividing curtains which are made as gifts from one tribal sheik to another. Further, the strips and pieces of a single curtain were sometimes woven by different tribes and these were then fitted together. As the curtain was constructed from its separate parts, so did the pattern become a physical embodi-

ment of the concept of unity between people. This kind of curtain is a special example of what has occurred in the history of Islamic pattern generally: the fusion of different influences, the assimilation of designs from different cultures.

Today the most richly patterned dividing curtains are rarely made or seen, and this type of weaving is on the decline; though use of the curtain does continue, and the ethic of hospitality in Bedouin life has not disappeared. But life has changed for nomadic people, and if they have benefited from twentieth century technology, they have also been forced to adjust to it. The art of pattern in nomadic culture has certainly been affected by manufactured synthetic textiles. One example is that Bedouin women no longer wear the **Thob'ob**, a combination of dress, underdress and veil with baggy folds; the

19

different layers insulated the body against heat and cold and the dress had embroidered zig-zag patterns. But today Bedouin women prefer a less voluminous dress made of artificial fibres. To survive, the old weaving ecology must compete with these same synthetic fibres. However, the painstaking process of spinning fleece, plying yarn, stringing the warp threads, and laboriously weaving and knotting by hand cannot compete with machine technology producing cheap, long-lasting products, even if the latter are aesthetically inferior to the old designs.

Design

Both tribal rugs and the more curvilinear pictorial court carpets consist of a central field and a border, the main border being accompanied by narrower bands known as guard stripes. The central field may be patterned by multiple repeats of a particular motif, or by a variety of motifs, or by a single main medallion, which may be floral or geometric, square, circular or rectangular. There are many medallion shapes which include spiral scrolls, clover leaves, flames, trefoils, and arabesques, showing how a certain carpet format is not restrictive but leads to variation and invention of pattern within the guidelines. In figurative carpets the field may be entirely occupied by a natural scene, often with a combination of viewpoints, so that the scene may be viewed from any side of the carpet, emphasising the essential non-illusionary devices of Islamic figuration. Alternatively, one or more figurative motifs may be set off against the coloured ground – for example, a vase, a row of cypress trees, a caravan of camels; the place held by such motifs in the pattern compostion necessarily gives them a rhythmic decorative function and such work, although figurative, does not work against the spirit of the Koran when it warns against the making of idolatrous images. In terms of structure, the repetition and variation of motifs in the central field may occur in horizontal, vertical or diagonal rows: these are the basic axes of regular design. A combination of axes gives the carpet its interrelation of devices within lattice structures. Carpets vary from the 'endless' repetition of motifs in rows, to designs based on the medallion which defines the inner field as a background, and against this sets up a system of connected, separated and 'echoed' motifs and medallions.

The pattern in Islamic rugs and carpets may be systematic, a network of uniform elements which do not depart from the set of rules by which each pattern is constructed; but still each carpet and rug is characterised physically by the method of working and the material employed, the number of knots per square inch, the variation in dyed colour, and the thickness of the piled yarn. These all play a vital part in the creation of the final work. Unpredictable physical variations do not deviate from the prescribed regularity of the design, but create certain irregular sensual refinements within the system. Sometimes there are variations in the shade of a particular dyed yarn, creating streaks in the carpet just where the design requires a repetition of the same colour. These **Abrasc**, however, are not regarded as faults, rather the luminous effects created are highly prized, enlivening the carpet ground and the surface of the wool. Additionally, such faults show the humility of all manufactured works, which must inevitably fall short of God's perfection.

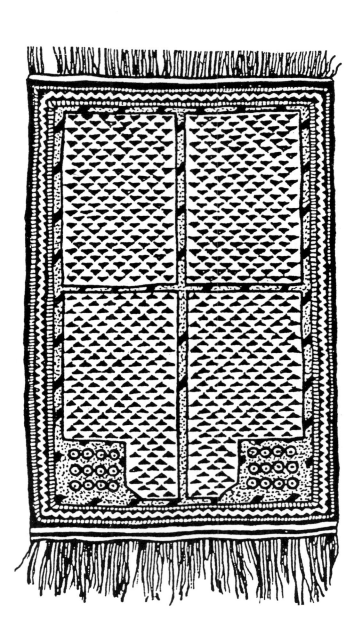

Above: This kelim with its radiating hooked design is a late 18th century/early 19th century work from Western Anatolia; it was the star exhibit in a kelim show held in London a few years ago. There is now an established market for kelims in Europe, where they are often used as floor rugs in the home, though in Islam they are primarily bed and furniture covers, or wall hangings.

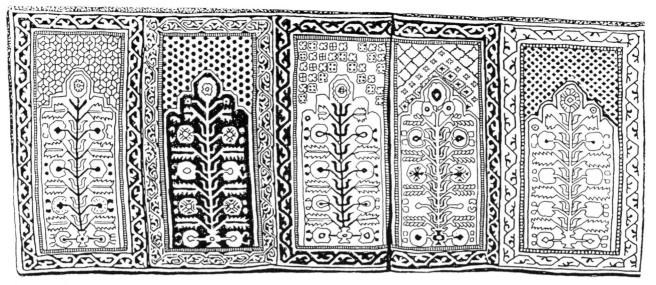

Above: A multiple prayer carpet: the rugs are joined together as those who pray are joined spiritually; this kind of carpet was often made of silk. Called the 'Samarkand' design, each mihrab contains a branching Tree of Life.

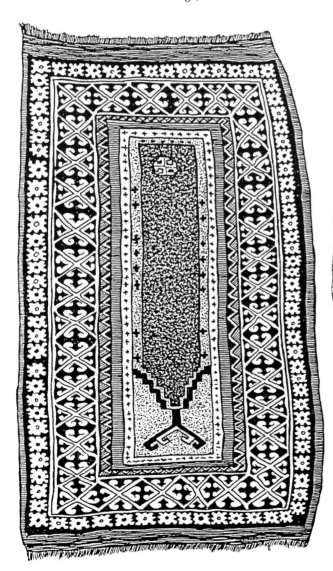

Above: The main field divided into four parts by a cross design is common to tribal rugs in Iran and Afghanistan. The patterns in the niches of the arch and the duck-egg blue colour of the cross and inner guard make this an unusual example.

Above: Madjur prayer carpet, made in 1860. Madjur is situated on the central plateau of Turkey and is noted for its prayer rugs, the borders of which are usually very wide and feature rhombus, star, Greek key and zig-zag patterns.

Colour

The yarn is dyed either by the weavers themselves or by a master dyer in a village or bazaar. Since the invention of aniline dyes in 1856, the art of dyeing using vegetables and animal substances has diminished. Artificial dyes have had a deleterious effect upon carpet production. They were for a long time prohibited in Iran since their lack of subtlety and radiance, and tendency to fade quickly, depressed the market. Today the synthetic colours are much improved, and at the same time the older, natural art is still practised. Wild madder root is used to make the various reds: the older the plant, the deeper the shade of red. Crushed cochineal insects make a bright magenta or a brilliant crimson when boiled in the dye vat. To make the vivid Turkey red, madder is mixed with milk which has been fermented for exactly thirty days. Ox blood is used to make brownish reds. All the vegetable-dye blues are made from the indigo plant. The depth of colour depends upon how often the wool is dipped into the dye to which fixatives such as honey or date have been added. Crocus, vine leaves, milkwort and buckthorn, walnut shells and pomegranate skins which are used to make carpet dyes also contribute to the floral iconography of pattern.

The symbolism of the colours in Islamic carpets varies according to the importance of the colours which are available in different areas. But it is possible to see a general picture. White represents peace, purity, and the colour of morning. Blue represents tranquility, associated with the night sky, reflections in water, eternity, thoughtfulness, meditation, high ideals and spiritual oneness. Red, on the other hand, is a powerful energetic colour signifying great joy, happiness, vitality, passion and other outgoing characteristics. Yellow is the colour of the sun and stands for glory, plenty, the riches of active power. Green is the sacred Islamic colour since it was the colour of Mohammed's banner, and the colour of the cypress, which was his favourite tree, being eternally green. Orange, used as the background colour in marriage-tree designs, signifies human love. Colours take on a particular significance through use and association. For example, purple is the colour of royalty because it was traditionally worn by the Shah; and so by extension purple comes to symbolise dreams which come true – the fabulous made a reality. The Sufis developed colour association and symbolism into a highly complex and sophisticated metaphysical system. But the emotional appeal of colour transcends even the beauty of Sufi analysis. Strong dark colours are used in the hot arid climate since all colour appears much weaker in very bright light, and at the same time these colours give relief to sun-tired, sun-dazzled eyes. Further, certain colours are powerfully evocative of a particular place, as with the soft turquoise colour found with-

out exception in Qum rugs, either in touches or as an entire background. This is also the colour of the rooftops in the holy city. This is a precise exact shade of blue which does not appear elsewhere in the cities of Islam.

Above: A Beshir rug from the border region between Turkmenistan and Afghanistan.

22

Knotting

The two principal knots used in rug-making are the **Persian Senneh** and the **Turkish Ghiordes.** The Senneh is a single knot made by passing the woollen strand under one warp, then over and around the next, so that the two ends of the pile show on either side of the warp thread. This knot can be made to face to the left or the right so that the lie of the pile can be in either direction. The Ghiordes is a double knot. It is made by looping the knot around two warp threads and bringing both ends of the wool out between them. The Turkish Ghiordes knot gives a firmer weave, although the single strand of the Persian Senneh knot allows far more flowing lines and apparently finer work because the knots occupy less space. Despite their names, the two knots are used throughout the rug-weaving world.

This knotting process is at least as old as the **Pazyryk** carpet which was made 2,500 years ago; the technique has remained essentially the same throughout Asia over two and a half millenia. Threads are stretched on a loom, the pile is knotted to these threads, and when a row of knots is complete, a weft thread is inserted to hold the knots in place – this is the essence of the ancient art of knotting a carpet. Although it is slow and painstaking work, this technique has survived because it provides a firm structural tension for hard-wearing fabric, and at the same time the introduction of differently coloured knotting threads makes possible a systematic creation of patterns. In this way we can see that the practical requirements of carpet making are inseparable from the way pattern is constructed: the pattern is not applied to the artefact, rather the pattern is structurally embodied in the carpet.

Above: Ghiordes mid-18th century knotted wool prayer carpet showing two pillars and a hanging oil lamp: the architectural space of the mosque is translated into a two dimensional design.

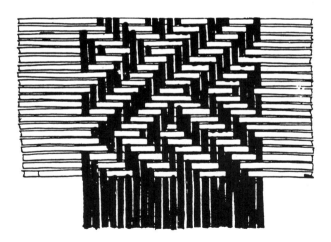

Left: Luristan rug woven by the nomadic Luri tribe from the mountainous areas of south-west Iran. This is a typical example of Luri geometric work with its three diamond motifs joined together by a stepped diagonal design. This, with the bright, luminous colours creates a bold striking effect. Luri rugs often have a Greek key pattern around the motifs in the central field. The Greek key is an ancient pattern which probably originated in simple mat weaving using dried grass and strips of leaf and bark (above). The design was carved on ivory ornaments in the Ukraine 15,000 years ago.

23

The Loom

The most common type of loom used by nomadic weavers in the Middle East is the horizontal loom: like all looms it is designed to hold the warp threads tight while the weft threads are interlaced through them and knots inserted. As the horizontal loom has a fixed heddle, the warp threads cannot be moved up and down mechanically to form passages for the weft, and consequently the process is laborious and tiring. The advantage of this loom, however, is that the warp is strung in a continuous length between the front and back beam of the loom, so that the work may be unpegged from the loom at any stage of the process, and the loom can be dismantled when the nomads travel on. The width of the woven piece is determined by the reach of the weaver, while the length desired determines the distance between the beams which are to be pegged. This kind of weaving is most often done by women and young girls, though in some tribes it may be the responsibility of men and boys; the latter in any case may repair and tassel carpets, and at some stage most of the tribal group will be involved in preparation of yarn and dyes, in cleaning and ironing, and in transport and bartering. From this we can see that the loom and the weaving process are central to the tribal way of life: the activity not only provides useful artefacts, it also reflects a way of life.

Room-sized carpets are generally made in the towns in **kar-hanehs**. Kar-haneh, the Persian word for workshop, is not a factory but a kind of workshop with lines of weavers working at vertical looms and a salim who calls the knots and helps to give a rhythm to the weaver's actions. Each kar-haneh has a master knotter who is the most important person in the workshop with authority over the looms and is responsible for all the materials used. If it is a large workshop there are several master knotters who hire the weavers, call the knots, and assist with the important parts of the weaving. Densely knotted and elaborately flowing designs, with 300 to 500 knots per square inch, come from the kar-hanehs. Such work can include perfectly woven circles, impossible on horizontal tribal looms where the lower knot count of 90 to 150 creates stepped weaving designs.

Traditional tribal patterns are passed on from mother to daughter, while in the bazaar there are carpet designers who refine designs and even invent new ones. This practice is related to the development of arabesque carpet design by book illustrators in 16th century Isfahan, when new kinds of carpet design were made for Shah Abbas and the royal courts. This transposition of a drawn design – a carpet cartoon – into a carpet is made as a kind of graph which shows the different areas of coloured knots required: these drawings are cut into strips and each strip tucked into the warp threads when it is required, the weaver looking up to follow the drawn instructions. This is quite different from the tribal memory procedure, just as the hierarchy of the kar-haneh is socially distinct from the group tribal activity. The pattern diagram is not only bought in the bazaar, it is to some degree an invention outside the history of the family group, a quite different relation being made between pattern and people: the inventor becomes a customer.

The horizontal loom used by nomadic weavers requires great physical effort: alternate sets of warp threads cannot be moved up and down mechanically to make passages for the weft, and instead the 'shed' must be made with muscle power alone. The women in the illustration above are working on a vertical loom in Iran: their learned skills are now employed in organised commercial weaving centres. The women work in easier conditions, and the vertical loom does not demand such hard physical work as the horizontal loom, but weaving still requires great concentration and dexterity. The women weave from a carpet plan, a drawn design which they follow; the woman below caries all the information for her carpet in her memory: it was taught her by her mother.

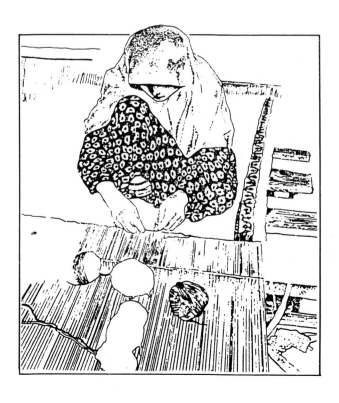

Motifs

The role of picturing is subservient to composition in Islamic design: figurative motifs work as parts of a system. At the same time, certain devices which may seem quite abstract, such as the swastika, circle, star, cross and diamond, have symbolic meaning, sometimes culturally specific and sometimes carrying a number of associational meanings. The mihrab, the khamsa, the hanging oil lamp, and the water jug, all have acquired religious meaning in Islam through direct reference to ritual and mosque. Other motifs are more ancient, such as the Tree of Life which is found in many parts of the world; but again, in Islam this image is bound up with a special history and geography, deriving from the story of the Tree of Life in Ancient Assyria: where a mystical eagle landed on the **Hoama**, the Paradise Tree of Life, breaking branches and scattering seeds. This image symbolizes the scattered people of the Islamic world, who are seeds of the same tree. To taste the juice of the Hoama is to become immortal; and the tree which links Islamic people in the Moslem faith with its five branches is depicted on Hajj murals, symbolizing the Five Duties. Tree of Life prayer carpets from Tuisserkhan in the Alvand mountains show the tree with tiny human figures as its fruits, making this interpretation clear.

As well as the tribal **gul** which is an emblem of the group and also works as a form of protective magic, carpets in Islam are covered in flowers – gardens for deserts where there are no flowers, and reminders of the Gardens of Heaven described in the Koran. The carnation, the tulip, the lotus, the lily, the rose, the chrysanthemum, together comprise a kind of 'language of flowers', bound up with the secrets of the dyer's art, and with tribal medicines and potions. The mir-i-boteh motif means 'princely flower', just as gul is etymologically derived from 'flower' in Persian. The mir has many interpretations: it is a flower, a flame, a seal hand-print, the pattern of the jewels in the Shah's crown, a winding bend of the Indus River, the pattern of a kashmir shawl, a cypress tree, a fir cone, half of the Chinese Yin-Yang symbol. Found throughout Islam, the mir demonstrates how pattern may be endlessly repeated not only as visual experience, but also symbolically. Motifs may be continually reinterpreted with different associations.

Above: Flower carpet by the Bakhtiari tribe with stylized flowers. The geometric motifs are reflected upon themselves.

Right: 19th century Shirwan Talish carpet from the Caucasus. The central field is filled with eight-pointed stars, a design common to Talish works.

25

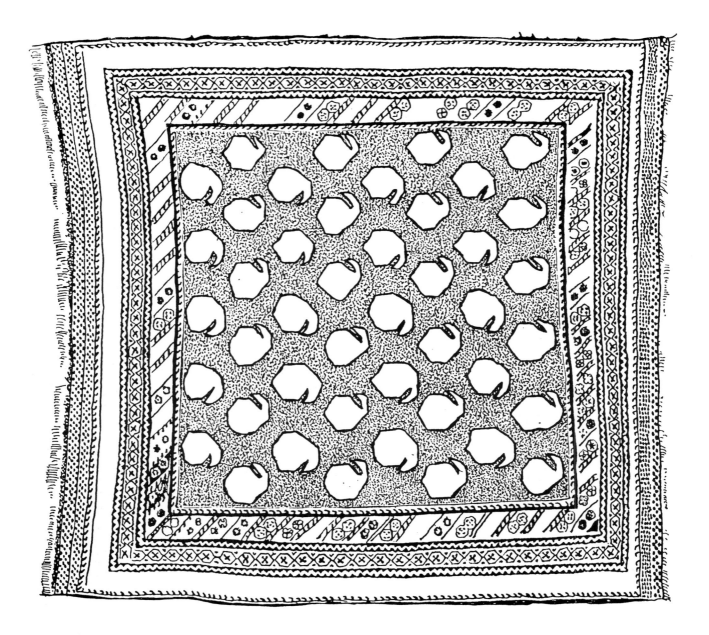

Above: Symbolic Miri-boteh design – 'princely flower'.

Court Carpets

Carpets in Islam may be classified according to the conditions of their production. The four general categories are: Tribal; Cottage Industry; Workshops; and Court. The Court carpet was made by weavers working with illuminators of manuscripts and books: this must have arisen from a desire to create carpets with the kind of intricate, intertwined detail familiar from patterned Korans. This must be seen as applied design, the art of the book being transposed to woven fabric. Shah Abbas the Great (1587 – 1629) replanned and rebuilt the city of Isfahan with his architect and engineer Sheikh Bahai from around 1597. The new splendid buildings, and the restoration of the Friday Mosque and the Minaret of Ali, created a need for carpets to adorn the interiors. Shah Abbas brought skilled weavers to the city, where they lived in a special district; they were to create carpets of quite a new type, splendid arabesque works with twining foliage and elegantly drawn animals. This enterprise, though its results were unique, was prophetic of the way in which demand would lead to the organisation of large manufactories working on planned designs. The new bazaar route led for over a mile between the Friday Mosque to the Maidan-i-Shah, and incorporates to this day the bustle of business in hundreds of small shops, with arched entrances leading to the mosques, little gardens and open squares, 'havens of tranquillity'. Here the trade in tribal and cottage industry rugs thrived under Shah Abbas's reign as the city grew wealthy. The picture is one of commercial rug dealing in the bazaar , whilst in the **Chahar Bagh**, the formal 'Four Gardens' which follows in straight lines the twisting and turning axis of the bazaar route, the carpet was laid out for relaxation, meditation and prayer in the garden pavilions. Some of Isfahan's carpets reflect the systematic, formal planning of the Chahar Bagh, whilst others with their interlacing arabesques recall the dynamism of the bazaar route. Saeb, court poet to Shah Abbas, described the city of Isfahan at this time: 'Each of its bricks is as valuable as a treasure, its jasmine gardens dawning in the heart of the night'. The Court carpets produced in 17th century Isfahan must owe much of their poetry to the excitement of the magnificent new city, as well as to the inventive nature of the new designs. Today, one may still stroll through the bazaar and the gardens, and re-enter the worlds of commerce and meditation, distinct and yet both essential to the carpet. Shopkeepers display tiles, carpets, jewellery, brassware and block-printed textiles, which in their great variety of patterns testify to the importance of pattern in Islamic culture at all levels of artistic production. And the formality of the ceremonial avenue

of the Chahar, flanked by its ordered gardens and the systematic course of streams, reveals much of the essential taste in the garden carpet.

The influence of engraved mirror designs, paper applique wall coverings, and stencil printing should not be overlooked: they too demonstrate how the gathering together of flourishing crafts leads to the exchange of designs, both in a planned way and unconsciously. We can say that the arabesque form, in mirror glass, on a page of the Koran, in an Isfahan carpet or on the wall of a residence, is the pattern form which transcends the limitations of all media to become one of the main contributions of Islam to design.

Below: Details of a large garden carpet. Zig-zag pattern expresses water. Stylized fish swim against the current. Pathways to flowers complete the scene.

27

The carpet is made by hand, and in a world of technological expertise the survival of the art must come through a recognition of the distinction between craftwork and mechanical process. The recognition does exist, both in the West and the East, so that the changes in colour of a dyed wool, the improvisation and deliberate mistakes of the weaver, the particular tension of the warp in a piece, are seen to establish uniqueness as both a crucial aspect of the aesthetic experience, and as an investment value. Hand weaving has survived the invention of the power loom, aniline dyes, and now computer technology: this is due to both increased awareness of the beauty of carpet pattern in Islam, and to the financial value now attached to a labour-intensive process. Unfortunately, in all too many centres of carpet production, costs of this complex process have only been kept down by the use of child labour at pitiful wages.

If such a form of innovation in the face of change gives us pause for reflection, it can nevertheless be argued that the Islamic design tradition still remains. In this way it parallels contemporary Japan where modern production techniques still employ traditional design concepts.

Right: An Arabic cut-out and appliqued paper wall covering from the 18th century. The art of paper cutting was cultivated during the 11th century by the shadow theatres of the Orient. In Turkey during the 16th century there was a craft guild of those 'who make all sorts of carved work out of paper'. In 1582, as the guild of Constantinople filed past the Sultan, the paper carvers exhibited 'a very beautiful garden and a castle decorated with flowers made of multicoloured papers, artistically carved'.

Below: Folding paper squares and rectangles (double folds and quadruple folds) and cutting out a design brings out the essential concept of symmetry in Islamic patternings.

3. Japanese Design

3. JAPANESE DESIGN

If Islamic design takes delight in complexity, it could be argued that simplicity and cleanness of line have a central place in the Japanese design aesthetic. Whilst the Islamic world has traditionally supplied one of the most basic commodities for the industrialized world, gasoline, Japan has in the last few decades become one of the world's principal suppliers of finished high-technology goods. Nevertheless, these industrial products develop from the traditions of Japanese design.

In Japan, pattern and stylization, not only in the visual arts but in custom, etiquette and attitudes of mind, can be seen as evidence of an underlying desire to come to terms with the natural world. Value is placed on both the visual and the sensuous impact of an object taken as a whole, whether it is a simple woven basket, the pattern inherent in the process of production, or a highly decorated lacquer box. The cultural aspects of the tea ceremony are a reflection of this total approach to environment, encompassing architecture, garden and interior design, dress, utensils and behaviour.

Japanese design has its base in the physically insecure environment of the islands. Because of earthquakes, volcanoes, landslides, typhoons, and tidal waves – a constant threat to survival – the Japanese have developed an acute awareness of natural phenomena and learned to adapt themselves to change in their environment.

Japan is an extremely mobile civilisation that has experienced numerous struggles against nature. Therefore physical culture has developed to be replaceable, renewable, or portable. The methods of packaging protect items of value for storage while remaining small and light enough to be easily carried. The **furoshike** (carrying cloth) is a good example of an economical method of transporting items. The cloth can be folded and packed away when not in use, so occupying the minimum of space.

The acute lack of space in Japan (a land with a large population in a small area) has had a great effect on every aspect of Japanese daily life. The maximum use of the minimum space is well illustrated by the interior design of Japanese houses. Interior space is partitioned by **hoji** (sliding doors made of thin wood and covered with translucent paper) and sometimes by folding screens. Room functions are totally interchangeable, daily activities and sleeping can be done in the same area, the **futons** (mattresses) being stored in a closet during the day. **Tatami** (straw mats) cover the floors and determine the dimensions of a room. A standard **tatami** mat is 6ft x 3ft and room sizes are given in mats: a six mat room, a two mat room.

Continuity and Adaptability

Continuity is also emphasised both in the adaptability of artifacts and the patterened arrangements upon them. In the West, beauty is usually framed or made up into a complete entity that is set up as adornment to daily life. In contrast to this, Japanese expressions of the aesthetic sense are based upon rearrangements of life's ordinary or daily items into a form that shows their natural beauty and enhances their overall environment. There is less sense of imposed form than in the West. The construction of the **Kimono** from straight strips of cloth displays this approach. Because the lengths of fabric continue from front to back without shoulder seams, unless the **Kimono** has a geometric pattern, the front and back of the design are reversed. The pattern appears continuous and boundaries are uncertain.

The world of Japanese beauty is the world of the incomplete. The emphasis upon the continuity of form is related to the concept of **nagare**, 'flow' (flow of life). In **Shinto**, Japan's national religion, the emphasis is upon the positive effects of change and renewal. For instance in gardens, geometrically executed formations would seem to the Japanese less a place of repose than a rigid mathematical demonstration. The perfect form asks our admiration rather than our participation.

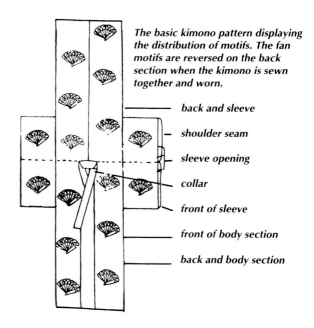

The basic kimono pattern displaying the distribution of motifs. The fan motifs are reversed on the back section when the kimono is sewn together and worn.

back and sleeve

shoulder seam

sleeve opening

collar

front of sleeve

front of body section

back and body section

Asymmetric Arrangement

In any arrangement of forms the Japanese favour the asymmetrical. This seems to be derived from their close observation of nature and its display of chance ordering; flowers appear where seeds fall, bushes and plants do not grow in straight lines, and rocks and stones do not have squared edges. Perfect symmetry, then, is avoided in a composition because flawless and matched designs lack movement and vitality. The aim in Japanese design is to extract the essence of nature and then express it in a simplified, even, symbolic form. Simplicity is favoured because the mystery of nature can only be suggested, and the simpler the suggestion, the greater its effectiveness. Thus an artistically created void in time or space becomes an important aesthetic consideration.

In all Japanese design, the motif is the dominant unit. It is often traditional and with literary overtones. The motifs are used as if they were part of a pattern book; they are kept intact within their perimeters but are moved about and adjusted in relation to other motifs. The final location of a motif seems almost always to be intuitive and based on the assumption of asymmetrical balance or tension. For example, the cartwheel motif is used in the kimono design where it is kept intact and adjusted in relation to the other motifs.

The **Shinto** faith particularizes nature with its many thousands of **kami** (anything that can inspire a feeling of awe, reverence or mystery) personifying individual units such as rocks, streams, caves and flowers. In this manner the uniqueness of individual units is accepted forming a sort of natural order of motifs.

The variety of Japanese design motifs is wide, and the range of applications is even wider. The same patterns, or closely related ones, appear on textiles, furniture, ceramics, weapons and architectural elements. The variety of decorative motifs can be explained by the Japanese conviction that the ornamentation of daily life is vital.

An example of the Juni-hitoe style.

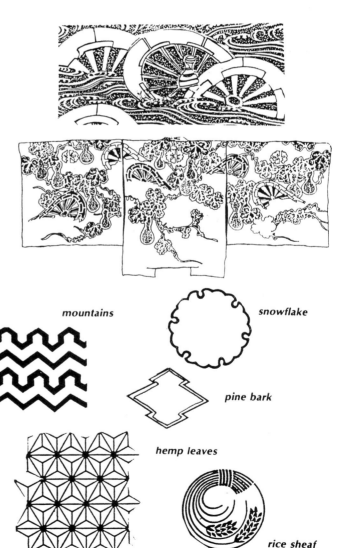

wisteria

waves

lightening

mountains

snowflake

pine bark

hemp leaves

rice sheaf

31

Living National Treasures

Japan produced legislation in 1950 to preserve traditional crafts by designating 'living national treasures', or more precisely, 'holders of intangible cultural properties'. This is unique in that it applies not only to tangible cultural properties like fine classic paintings and sculptures but also to invisible ones like techniques and skills of performing arts and crafts. As these techniques cannot exist without human beings embodying them, the law designates such persons as objects of protection. The Japanese government's cultural agency actively sponsors regular exhibitions and training courses for successors.

The singling out of individuals as holders of important skills in traditional arts and crafts is unique to Japan. No other nation seems to have valued the things of beauty in daily life in quite the same way. However, the decoration and the technique in which it is executed must be integrated with the form and function of the object. In Yanagi's words, *'every craftsman must consider three natural limitations: the purpose for which a given article is used, the nature of the materials employed, and the appropriate technique.'*

Japanese craftsmen have perfected techniques of carving, painting, lacquering, dyeing and weaving to give permanent expression to decorative motifs and always *'the disciplines of process decide the character of pattern'*. The popularity of certain motifs has remained fairly constant throughout the history of

Japanese arts and crafts; others have enjoyed a cyclical popularity fading out of fashion in one area only to reappear with renewed vigour and with modifications a few decades later.

The plum blossom has always been a popular deign motif in Japan. Because it is the first flower to bloom in spring, the plum blossom symbolises bravery. The motif was used as early as the Nara period and still appears in the Momoyama period fabric.

The Paulowina motif is used in many designs. Thses two examples show it interpreted in metalwork and

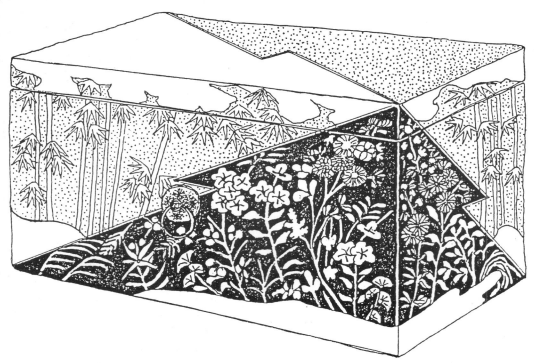

A momoyama lacquered stationery box displaying the zig-zag division of the ornamental area.

32

Patterns and Processes

Textile design is one area of the Japanese decorative arts in which both the traditional aspects of design and those aspects which mark the change of patron and market can be followed. To understand the value that was placed on the decoration of textiles for clothing, it is important to consider the place that the **kimono** had in Japanese life.

The Kimono

Standardised in its form, the kimono gains distinction and novelty from its decoration; a fine kimono was an adornment in the same way as jewellery. The garment is angular in its outline and presents flat areas where the detail of pattern may be displayed. The word Kimono (literally 'clothing') refers to the traditional wrap-around garment with rectangular sleeves worn by both men and women. It is made of vertical panels of cloth stitched together and is bound with an obi (a sash).

Generally kimonos are only worn now in Japan by a few people on formal occasions, although most people wear a casual **kukata** for relaxation, and elderly people do wear kimonos more regularly. However, a custom-made kimono is an original work by a creative artist and such a garment is likely to be handed down from one generation to the next, like a painting or a piece of jewellery.

Traditionally, a bride was given a set of kimonos on her wedding day which were meant to last a lifetime. But at the end of every ten years, the colours and designs of the facbric would have to change because the older the wearer, the darker the colours and the smaller the pattern would have to be. The kimonos would be unpicked, bleached, re-dyed, and then re-sewn.

This tradesman's coat shows the characters for 'fish market' and a design of a fish.

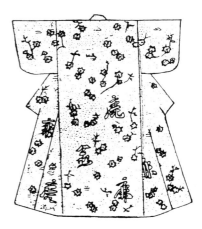

This kimono displays a bold use of the Ashide (characters in design) decoration. The character for deer is printed along with maple leaves, creating a striking effect.

A woman's favourite kimono was donated at her death to a temple. The priests cut these kimonos into patches to make their robes. This was a continuation of an ancient custom. When clothing material was scarce it was a widespread practice to patch small pieces of fabric together to make clothes. Buddhist priests made their **kesa** (or surplice) out of cast-away rags or fragements of material donated by the faithful. It was the custom for a man who had reached the age of sixty to be presented with a kimono made up from different pieces of material each given by a friend with good wishes for health and long life. The design potential of the patchwork technique was utilised in several ways (e.g. each half of a kimono being a different colour or design, a kimono divided into square sections alternatively filled with two different designs).

A kimono is made of straight strips of cloth about eighteen inches wide and loosely sewn together, so that it may be easily taken apart for cleaning or washing. The cotton kukata was often washed intact and hung on a bamboo pole run through the sleeves – a non-ironing process that antcipated drip-dry!

The kimono to some extent is a 'one size fits all' garment which developed to meet the requirements of the Japanese climate. The hot, humid summers required a loose-fitting, comfortable garment. The kimono with its large sleeves and ample size is airy for summer and can be made to fit for winter by adding layers.

This 'wrapping' phenomenon is a distinctive aspect of Japanese culture seen most dramatically during the **Heian** period (794 – 1185 A.D.) when ladies of the court donned many layers of kimono for ceremonial occasions. Known as **junihitoe**, the colour combinations of the layers were strictly regular and various combinations were given composite names. For instance, colours worn from February to March were known as 'shades of the plum blossom'.

The predecessor of the kimono is the **kosode** (small sleeves) which was worn as an undergarment from the Nara period, and as the outer garment of everyday apparel from the **Muromachi** period. Transfer of political power in the latter period from the nobility to the military samurai class who urged a life of simplicity and frugality was probably responsible for the popularity of the uncomplicated kosode.

But by the **Momoyama** period the kosode had become the object of elaborate textile designs, and was used by both men and women for extravagant display. This trend experienced a reversal when the Tokugawa shogunate came to power. In the **Edo** period every effort was made by the shogunate to stratify society and to perfect the feudal system as quickly as possible. The shogunate emphasised the necessity for people to behave in accordance with their class. Four main classes were distinguished: samurai, farmer, artisan and merchant. The wearing of dress unsuited to one's class was punished. In the Edo period the garment was used to convey a wide range of information about the wearer. It indicated the sex, age, marital status, class, rank or occupation of the wearer, as well as the season or an occasion of congratulations or condolence. Apart from slight variations in form, material and technique, the differences were shown solely by the kinds and colours of the kosode pattern.

However, even in this repressive age there were some situations in which a limited freedom remained. These were the licensed quarters and the theatre. These two environments became the centre of fashion, with courtesans and actors responsible for introducing new designs. The kosode represented a popularization of the outstandingly extravagant Noh costumes, nurtured under the patronage of the aristocracy.

A scene from a Noh play. The angularity of the garment was emphasised by using stiff brocades or several layers of highly decorative costumes.

The earliest Japanese textile patterns were created by a skillful manipulation of natural dye colours. From the simplest plain weave construction, an iridescent effect was achieved by using different colours in the warp and weft. Until the **Asuka** period colour manipulation continued to be the primary means of decoration.

Many intricately striking designs have been created by innovative dyeing techniques. Due largely to technical necessity, woven patterns tend to be geometrical. In order to decorate fabrics with more complex pictorial designs, the technique of double layer weaving (**Karaori**) was perfected, allowing weavers to produce patterns of birds and flowers. Because areas of coloured thread remained loose on the textile surface this weaving technique gave the effect of embroidery. Indeed, embroidery was often used in conjunction with woven or dyed designs to add contrasts of texture in patterns. Showing something of the flexibility of painting, it brought a feeling of depth to what would otherwise be flat areas of colour. Embroidery remained popular even when weaving and dyeing techniques became more sophisticated.

An asymmetric pattern, deliberately off-centre, creating a visual tension between motif and background.

The interlocking symmetrical design of a circular motif creates a dynamic effect. The repeat is delineated by the lines between the motifs.

The individual asymmetric motif is designed to end up in repeat to form a symmetric whole.

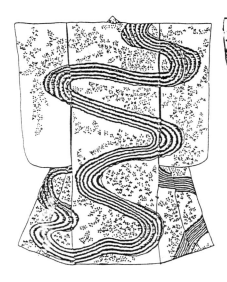

The random pattern's loose rhythms are created by flowing lines; the pattern is largely unstructured.

This deliberately incomplete design, like the asymmetric pattern, creates tension. It underlines the Japanese appreciation of the imperfect incomplete design

Abstract pattern: the regularity of this is derived from the process by which the fabric was made, i.e. the weft threads of weaving.

Gardens

The approach to a tea house was through a tea garden (**roji niwa**), the ideal of which was sought in the desolate tranquility of a mountain trail. Among the contributions of the tea garden to the contemporary Japanese garden are stepping stones, stone lanterns and groves of trees, as well as stone washbasins for guests being served tea.

There are four traditional styles of Japanese gardens. The **funa asobi** (pleasure boat) style: this centred on an oval-shaped pond, where courtiers went boating, and was a popular type of garden in the Heian period. The **shuyu** (stroll) style: a garden whose chief feature is a park leading from vantage point to vantage point from which changing scenes could be viewed. The **kansho** (contemplation) style: the garden is viewed from within a central structure, the emphasis being placed on the creation of a carefully composed scene suggestive of a picture and suitable for long and studied viewing. The **Kaiyu** (many pleasure) style: the garden was constructed around a central pond displaying striking changes of scene to the viewers.

There are three basic principles of scene composition: reduced scale, symbolization, and borrowed view. Reduction in scale refers particularly to the **kaiyu** style garden, which brings together in a confined area adaptations of famous scenes and places of historical interest through miniaturization of natural views of mountains and rivers. Symbolic forms include abstraction, as in the use of white sand to suggest the ocean, and inference, as in a grouping of stones or an island signifying the crane and tortoise. The term 'borrowed view' describes the use of background views outside and beyond the garden, such as a beautiful mountain, a broad plain, or the sea. These are used in such a way that they become part of the interior scenic composition.

Some gardens represent miniature versions of the Japanese landscape, the raked sand being the sea and the rocks the mountains. Gardens such as this inspired a contemplative attitude.

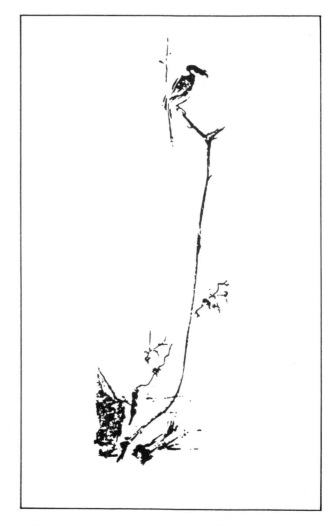

Shrike on a tree stump shows a particular bird caught at a specific point of time, as if a snapshot had been taken. It has been painted with as few marks as possible. But because the artist has concentrated upon the essential form of the bird and the basic structure of the tree, the painting could represent any bird or tree.

36

Packaging

Rituals of wrapping are very important in Japan. They are informed by three considerations:
- an aesthetic philosophy that believed everything should be made beautiful;
- a system in which all objects, large or small, expensive or cheap, were valued; and
- the ancient concept of cleanliness and uncleanliness.

Packaging purifies and distinguishes the contents of the package from all similar objects. Wrappings were developed from the natural world – in rural areas a given object was simply wrapped in whatever material lay at hand. The outcome was adequate for storing and transporting the object and both functional and simple in execution: bamboo leaves to hold rice dumplings, and knotted straw to carry eggs.

These materials were further developed by craftsmen who produced intricate and luxurious lacquer boxes, extravagantly patterned **fukusa** (woven or embroidered cloths used to cover boxes containing ceremonial gifts), and dyed furoshiki (square cloths tied horizontally by the corners and used to carry things around).

It is still the custom to wrap everything on every occasion: even money is wrapped before it is presented. Next to computerised cash dispensers in banks there is always a pile of decorated envelopes in which cash can be wrapped. The smallest **furoshiki** is 32 cm square, and is used for presenting money on formal occasions. Inside the cloth there is a rectangular board, lacquered red for festive occasions and black for funeral offerings. Large deep red cotton **furoshikis** decorated with symbols of longevity are used for wrapping wedding gifts.

The choice of exactly the right gift for the right occasion and person is governed by a complex system of ettiquette. Gifts must be given before New Year and at the start of summer, and all must be wrapped. They must never be unwrapped in front of the giver, or any mention made of the gift thereafter.

The elderly woman rests, her large furoshiki beside her. The furoshiki is still used in Japan today.

Organisation of Pattern

The most common features of Japanese pattern are an avoidance of symmetry and a rigidly structured system of repeat. When it does occur, symmetry is used as a device to lend authority to a motif, e.g. in family crests, or as a result of a repeat system which has developed it as a secondary factor in the design. Regular patterns such as stripes or checks are often developed from the technique of weaving.

Decisions about where to place motifs are not made according to any set rules of composition but are made on an intuitive basis. Any arbitrariness or seeming incompleteness of design which might result from such an approach is considered as a contributory feature rather than as a flaw in the design. This is compatible with the fact that the Japanese have lived with inconsistency in their natural environment and accepted it as a feature of life and an attribute to be developed in art.

Many of the decorative motifs used in Japanese design are deceptively casual in effect. For example, textile designs incorporate an abundance of motifs from everyday life and the natural environment as well as a variety of more abstract ones. Relatively few of these motifs are chosen for their decorative qualities alone. Many seemingly abstract patterns are either graphic symbols of a religious concept or extremely stylized naturalistic motifs which in their turn often represent a concept or value significant for the Japanese.

In the Edo period certain motifs gave an indication of a person's status either straightforwardly, as in the case of family crests, or less obviously in the use of symbolic motifs.

The Japanese experience extreme weather changes during the seasonal cycle, and significance was consequently given to seasonal motifs in the decoration of textiles, so a spring kimono might display a cherry blossom, a summer garment might be coloured in plum or azalea, autumn dress might be patterned with maple leaves or chrysanthemum flowers, winter pine trees or snow.

This tradesman's coat shows the characters for "fish market" and a design of a fish.

This kimono is a mixture of abstract lattice patterns and symbolic patterns of stylized lightning and eight spoke wheels. The image of lightning because of its fearsome associations, is one that was adopted by Samurai warriors, the eight Samurai Buddhist stages towards enlightenment.

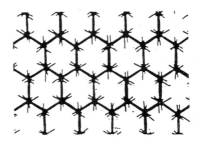

The hexagonal pattern is a network of tortoise shapes, symbolising, according to Japanese mythology, a long life.

38

Project Ideas

Trace a symmetrical design such as the one of the Japanese crafts shown below. Gradually shift the design to one side until more than one half is off the paper. How does the revelation of a large area of empty space change the effect of the design?

Find examples of different constructed fabrics, e.g. twill, corduroy, hessian. Study them to see what type of abstract pattern they might suggest. Make a patchwork of various patterns.

Design motifs you feel are appropriate for particular seasons.

Discuss abstract symbols that you are already familiar with. For example, what meanings do you attach to heart shapes, crosses, swastikas and sun symbols?

Create an abstract pattern using one such symbol by drawing a grid and repeating the symbol. If the shape is symmetrical, your pattern will create more interest if placed in a half-drop repeat grid. Patterns can be made from a combination of symbols.

The Japanese developed an attitude towards nature which led them to identify the qualities they valued in human life with the attributes of certain plants and animals. Discuss which animals you feel have a particular personality and make a design based on one of them. It may be useful to remember sayings such as 'as brave as a lion', 'as meek as a lamb', 'as quiet as a mouse', 'as loyal as a dog'.

Discuss the traditional ways that the Japanese express their personalities through their clothing and its decorations with the ways that Western fashions achieve this end.

The metal fitting of this Kamakura laquered box echoes the major fan motif.

Exercises in Simplification and Abstraction

All of the exercises require suitable still life objects or plants for the class to draw.

1) Restrict the time given for a pupil to finish his/her drawings, e.g. 3 – 5 minutes per drawing.

2) Restrict the means, e.g. place large sheets of paper on an easel or floor, tie large brush to the end of a stick.

3) Limit the number of marks the pupil is allowed to make, e.g. 5 – 6 per drawing.

4) Let the class study an object for a few minutes, then remove it, and ask them to draw it from memory.

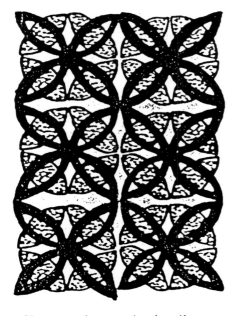

Shippo-tsunagi or seven jewel motif.

Nindo-mon or honeysuckle pattern.

Stencil Cutting

For this exercise in stencil cutting, it will be easier to print onto paper than fabric. The latter is considered later.

Study the examples of Japanese crests and swordguards. These are single units designed to be independent. There is a predominance of natural forms in the designs which reflects the Japanese reverence for nature.

Crests were first used by the aristocracy to mark their possessions and then by military families on the battlefield. By their highly simplified nature crests reduce common motifs to their essential components. Use a motif or motifs that are personally significant to design a crest or a 'logo' for yourself that reflects your interests. A successful logo will be instantly recognisable or eye-catching, it could be used as a means of identification – a badge or a letterhead. Your design need not be necessarily confined to the shape of a circle. Draw your design onto a piece of card (approx. 15cm X 15cm). Before you start to cut, consider the positive and negative areas – take care not to cut out areas that may fall away from the main piece of card.

Here are a couple of ideas for crest designs. The clasped hands represent friendship, the letters could be your initials.

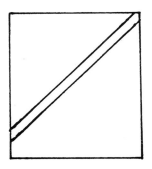

This will fall apart.   *The bridges will hold this in place.*

The stencils demonstrate various approaches to design. In a previous worksheet you have made a simplified study, base your stencil on this drawing.

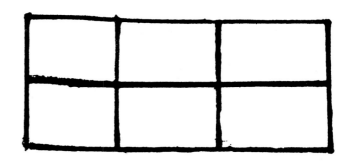

block repeat

Take   piece of flexible thin card (about 6" square). Draw your design on to it using the whole area.

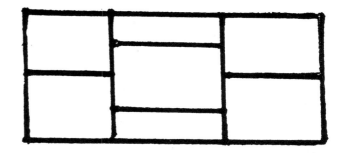

half drop

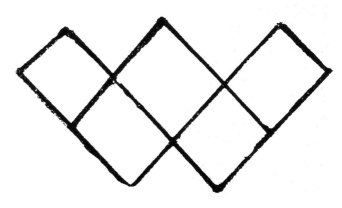

diamond repeat

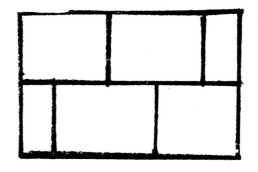

After a stencil has been cut consider the various ways to arrange it. You may want to turn the stencil so it is not all pointed the same way around.

brick repeat

Examine these stencils carefully. The dark areas are paper and the white areas are spaces.

This thistle design is one of a series of stencils to be over-dyed with several colours to complete the image.

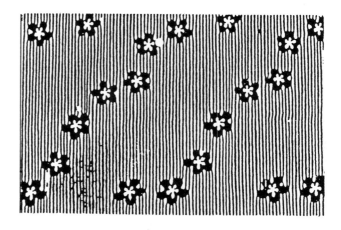

Plum blossom against a faded winter sky. The dark and light areas are a result of varying width of lines.

The crane is very popular design motif in Japan. It symbolizes longevity and is often used on formal kimonos as a family crest. Japan Airlines have adopted a simplified version of the crane.

42

Kasuri Weaving

Kasuri is a technique in which lengths of thread are tied and dyed before weaving.

The word Kasuri comes from the verb *kasureru* which means 'to blur'. Kasuri may have developed independently in Japan as well as being assimilated from Indonesia where it is known as **Ikat**. Basic Kasuri patterns are cross and parallel cross designs. More complex Kasuri are pictorial and are known as **E-gasuri**.

Teacher's Notes

Discuss the notion of Kinetic pattern – the image is not static – there is a suggestion of movement. The idea that the pattern is created through process-preliminary planning on paper is not necessarily needed. Natural dyestuffs from onion skins, food colouring, etc., could be used to dye the threads.

The concept of the distortion of a geometric design is indicative of Japanese love of the unbalanced or incomplete.

Paper Weaving

You will need two pieces of paper. On a rectangle make a simple but bold design. Now cut this sheet of paper into strips.

These are weft threads.

Take a square piece of paper and make cuts vertically down the sheet. Leave a band of uncut paper at the top and bottom of the sheet.

This is the warp.

Now weave the weft strips under and over the warp. Experiment with changing the pattern by pulling the weft threads different ways.

Perhaps you could draw the same motif on both sheets of paper in different colours.

An Adaptation of the Kasuri Technique using Rainbow Wool

Take a piece of stiff card 30cm X 10cm. With a Stanley knife cut 25 notches about 1cm apart. Make the notches directly opposite each other with an extra notch at the end.

Wind a piece of wool tightly around all the notches. Sellotape the ends onto the card. These are your warp threads.

Choose a ball of rainbow wool cut into lengths. Thread through the warp with a weaving needle. Leave plenty of spare wool at either end. Try to align the colours on top of each other. According to the way the weft is pulled, the design will take shape.

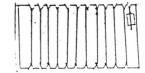

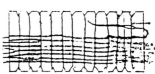

Do not weave too tightly. Push the weft threads well down onto each other so that the warp threads do not show through.

Paper

Handmade paper or **Washi** is highly prized in Japan. The papers are valued for the striking ways in which they are decorated. One process used in the decoration of Washi is tie-dyeing. The process described below is an adaptation of the traditional technique.

Procedure:

1) Take a sheet of paper and fold to double thickness.
2) Fold or pleat the paper.
3) Soak the loosely tied or untied paper in water. Greaseproof will benefit from having boiled water poured over it and soaked for 30 minutes. Cartridge paper needs only 5 minutes in cold water. This gives the final design a softer look.
4) Pat off excess water.
5) Carefully attach the binding or clips.
6) Immerse in the dye bath until a good colour is achieved.
7) Take the bundle out of the dye and pat off excess moisture and allow to dry.
8) When the bundle has dried for a while carefully undo it. Soak up any excess dye with cloth.

Tye-dyed Paper

Types of Paper

Various types of paper can be used but start with a medium absorbency paper– greaseproof, cartridge, typing paper, envelopes or newsprint. The dyeing time may vary from 15 minutes to several hours or more according to absorbency. Soft and very absorbent paper needs only a short while in the dye, but has to be handled with great care.

Folding and Pleating

Avoid folding the paper too sharply; knife-edge creases can be weak spots. It is usually necessary to fold the paper double before pleating.

Binding

Fold or pleat the paper and then tie with rubber bands, string, cloth pegs, paper clips, or bulldog clips. Make the ties quite wide to ensure there is a resist area.

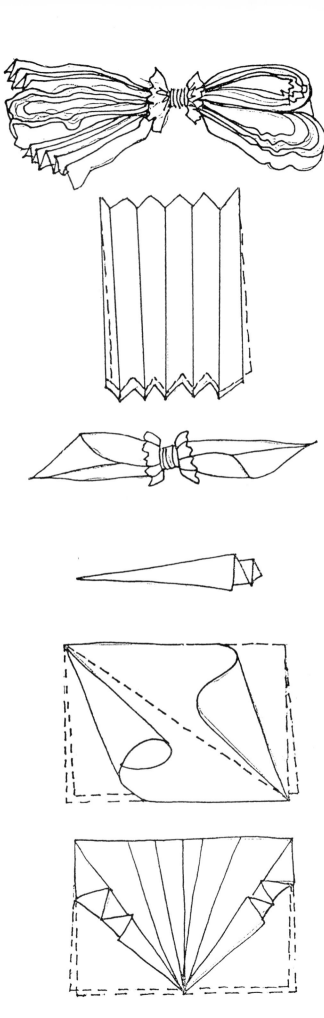

Gold Stater. Geometric design derived from a mural wreath, 1st Century BC.
BIRMINGHAM MUSEUMS and ART GALLERY

4. Celtic Design

Celtic Design

The third cultural design system chosen as an example for this book differs from the previous two in that it represents an indigenous Western minority culture with links which stretch across Europe to the Middle East.

The two strands of Celtic identity, language and material culture, appeared on the European stage at different times. The introduction of ironworking techniques was the spur to the development of a recognisable Celtic culture but this was grafted on to an existing structure where people may have been speaking a form of Celtic language as early as 2,000 BC.

The art of Bronze Age Europe and early Celtic culture shows a distinct continuity (which probably also indicates a continuity in religious belief). Both use a geometric style of simple repeat patterns with straight lines and circles making decorative bands of chevrons, lozenges, triangles and circles. The spiral is also a commonly used motif.

A series of major upheavals in the Near East disturbed the relatively peaceful lives of Bronze Age Europeans. In the twelth and thirteenth centuries BC the Hittite Empire of Central Turkey, which had kept a strict monopoly of ironworking technology, collapsed, sending people fleeing into Europe with their valuable skills.

By the eighth century BC, a change was seen in the burial customs of Central Europe. Whilst the majority of people continued to be cremated and the remains placed in pottery urns, chieftains were now distinguished by being buried with their belongings in wooden chambers within large earthen barrows. This distinct culture is known as **Hallstatt** from the first archeological site found in the Austrian Alps during the nineteenth century.

From these grave goods of the Hallstatt period we can see all the elements of Celtic art coming together for the first time. The Hallstatt Celts, with their native resources of iron and salt deposits, took advantage of their position on the major trade routes from the Near East and the Mediterranean.

Roman coin showing a Celtic chariot-team in action.

Bronze situla with repoussé relief

The process of ironworking was the most important Near-Eastern influence. Iron was mainly used for sword blades, conferring an immediate superiority over bronze in warfare. Iron could also be used wherever there was constant wear and tear. Gold and bronze were the more flexible materials and could be hammered into thin sheets, cast, cut or moulded, so that they remained the mainstay of artistic expression.

The practice of burial also came from the Near East, while the widespread use of horses was probably intoduced by the Scythians and Cimmerians, nomads from the southern Russian steppes.

A characteristic of Hallstatt burials is the presence of bronze buckets ('situlue') decorated in repoussé, where bands of figures and animals have been ham-mered out from the back, and whose style also shows an oriental origin. The other main influence was from imported Greek wine vessels which were highly prized by the Celts. Yet, despite being familiar with the narrative figure-style of Greek pottery, the Celts chose not to incorporate it in their own art. Instead they became fascinated with the minor floral designs like the decorative borders of palmettes flanked by lotus flowers, and continued developing variations of this theme with tireless ingenuity and skill for centuries.

Throughout their independent history, inspiration for their art continually came from beyond the Celtic world. Established as they were in the millenia-old tradition of northern Europe, the Celts took those images that already fitted into their way of seeing the world, and which favoured the symbolic over the naturalistic. The idea behind the image was always of greater importance than the image itself, and reflected the importance attached to imagination, puns and riddles.

It was inevitable that such a fundamental difference between the Celtic mind and the rational Classical cultures of the Mediterranean would lead eventually to serious clashes.

Gold bowl showing pre-Celtic motifs, from a Hallstatt tomb

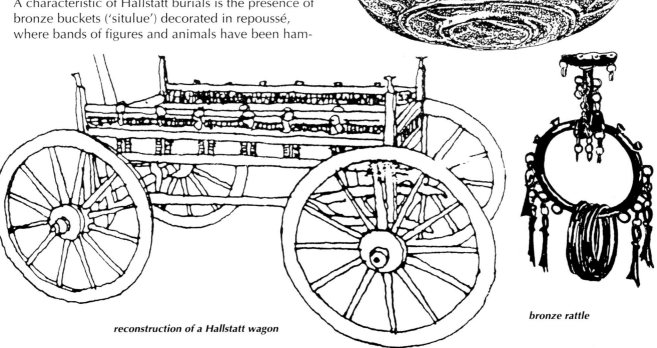

reconstruction of a Hallstatt wagon

bronze rattle

Celtic Christianity

The Christian conversion of Ireland began during the fifth century AD when the rest of Western Europe was entering the five hundred years of confusion, known as the 'Dark Ages'. Germanic tribes had swept across Europe from the East, forcing the Romans to strengthen further their northern and eastern borders. As the pressure increased the legions were gradually withdrawn from Britain, leaving the eastern shoreline vulnerable to the attacks of Angles, Saxons and Jutes from across the North Sea. A series of coastal defences was established by the remaining Roman governors, but they had little chance of preventing these invaders from settling. Only Ireland and the remote parts of north Britain remained isolated from these disturbances.

During these centuries the Celts, now isolated from the Continent, developed an art based upon their newly acquired Christian faith. Although an ornamental art, it never wholly lost touch with the reality of nature, and was akin to the world of magic where familiar shapes and ideas are used in unfamiliar surroundings. In this art the ordered geometrical framework is camouflaged by a profusion of symbolic imagery. Before considering the art in detail, it is necessary to understand the background against which its transformation and later development took place.

In Irish society, tribal chieftains handed on power by the rules of succession. Druids controlled religious faith while an order of jurists (**brehons**) were the guardians of law. The poets (**bards**) played an important part in society and their training took up to twenty years. They learnt how to recite poems, often thousands of lines in length, and combined history and current events in a vast oral mythology. The bard would travel from kingdom to kingdom praising the virtue of the king and making favourable comparisons with other kings. Each king treated the bard well, because the use of satire could destroy a king's standing in the eyes of the people. In a society with such an oral tradition the druids played a fundamental role in the keeping of schools for learning, and they opposed the Christian missionaries.

Carpet page from the Book of Durrow

48

Christianity had been introduced into southern parts of Ireland by the churches of Britain as early as the end of the fourth century, but it was only during the following century that organised missions appeared, the best known of which was St. Patrick's.

The historic writings tell of his captivity in pre-Christian Ireland, his escape, and then of his return to preach the gospel.

It would seem that the missionaries became established by accepting and adapting certain old beliefs and secular customs. The church was adopted by many tribal kings who gave land in return for its blessing. This compromise resulted in new life for old Celtic traditions while a distinct Celtic church gradually developed.

For the first time a written alphabet known as **Ogham** was developed. It was simple and usually incised on both edges of a rough burial stone and often accompanied by Latin inscription. The Druids had used secret languages, for example using leaves of different trees to represent letters and stringing them together to send messages to each other.

Ogham may be derived from a sign language where fingers were placed across the shin or arm.

During this period western sea routes remained open and the wine trade flourished, bringing to western parts of the British Isles fine pottery from North Africa. Along with this came the knowledge of a new monastic way of life, intensely Egyptian (Coptic) in origin. During the sixth century many monasteries were built and the church assumed more and more the function of leading the people in intellectual and artistic activities. The missionaries had brought with them books and sacred objects, chalices, bells and new knowledge in metal working and masonry. New objects and buildings appeared and traditional Celtic patterns were incorporated in their decoration.

St. Columcille (St. Columba), among others, was responsible for building many monasteries and churches, choosing to build on ancient religious sites such as oak groves. The most important of these foundations was at Durrow (Plain of Oaks), which became a centre of scholarship and spirituality renowned throughout Europe.

Greek decorated pottery was the inspiration for much Celtic design

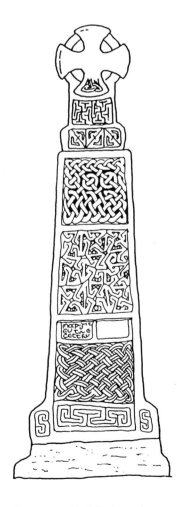

Carew cross Dyfed, eleventh century

Detail of the Book of Kells

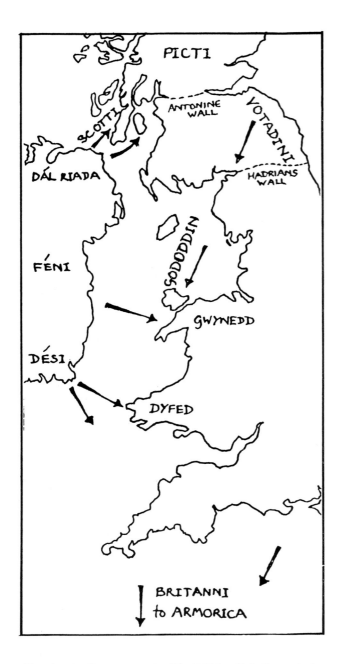

By the late sixth century illuminated manuscripts such as the 'Cathach' were being made, possibly by St. Columba himself. In this book the decoration was restricted to initials that adapted Celtic scroll motifs from metalwork and new types of stylised animal ornament which had been developed from late Roman patterns by the Germanic and Norse peoples. A Coptic influence is evident in the surrounding red dots. Only half of this Psalter has survived which is a miracle in itself as it was used as a talisman by the O'Donnell chiefs during their battles with other tribes! St. Columba also dictated how poets should compose and how metalworkers should use ornamental motifs credited with supernatural powers.

The artists worked within the monastery, which was a group of simple buildings surrounded by a protective wall and ditch, among which was a 'scriptorium', where manuscripts were written.

For the Celtic artists the vellum surface offered new possibilities. Each book of the Gospels would be filled with a symbolism drawn from a vast oral mythology, kept alive round the fires of Hallstatt and Le Tene chieftains. In the writing and embellishing of certain portions of scripture no effect was spared in making the text a thing of great visual beauty. Indeed, Christians saw such devoted workmanship as an act of worship to God.

Processes included the use of brilliant and durable colours which were obtained from seashells and plant juices. Designs were, in many cases, geometrically designed for a certain space or page. Vellum pages were made from animal skins such as calf. The skin would be soaked in limewater for 3–4 weeks until the hairs fell out, and after drying in the sun, was smoothed with a stone before the illuminator could set to work.

Map showing the movements of the British celts in the centuries after the withdrawal of the last Roman legions.

A Roman coin showing the head of a Celt with long swept-back hair.

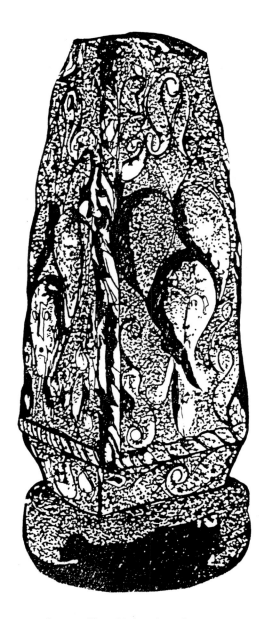

Above: Carved stone pillar with four faces from Germany, c. 400 BC

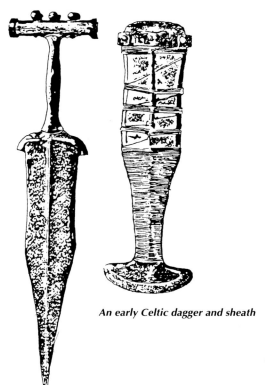

An early Celtic dagger and sheath

Art flourished under the patronage of the Celtic Church, and one of the main figures to play a role in the church's growth was St. Columba. Following Ninian, who had founded the first monastic settlements in Scotland, he arrived in exile from Ireland on Iona, off the west coast of Scotland, in 653 AD. From this base he began to make converts in all the Kingdoms of northern Britain, and by the end of the sixth century Iona was the most important monastic house in the north.

In the early seventh century another influential monastic community was established on the island of Lindisfarne in Northumbria by monks from Iona, and this brought the Celtic church into direct conflict with the Roman church which had steadily gained control of southern Britain since the arrival of St. Augustine in England in 597 AD. Irish missionaries had already travelled across the continent setting up monasteries at Luxeuil in France, St. Gall in Switzerland, and even crossed the Alps to found a monastery at Bobbio in northern Italy. The Roman Church saw the Celtic Church as not only a rival for power, but also a misguided establishment that needed to be brought into line with the rest of Europe.

The main differences, such as the computation of the date of Easter and other festivals, the structure of the priesthood and the liturgy, had come about through the blending of the druidic and Christian teachings and many of the Celtic monks had received druidic or bardic training. Even St. Columba had been taught within this tradition, and argued eloquently for the maintenance of the colleges of bards in Ireland. The Celtic churches gradually lost ground and after 630 AD only Iona, Lindisfarne and other Columban monasteries in Scotland and Ireland continued to resist the change to Roman rule. At Whitby in 644 AD the Northumbrian king voted to adopt the Roman liturgy, and as a result Celtic missionaries gradually withdrew from Lindisfarne.

There is little obvious prior work to the appearance of the 'Book of Durrow' in the second half of the seventh century, but it does show the great strides made by the illuminators. It also beautifully illustrates the value of the blank space for showing up designs, later found in such metalwork as the Ardagh Chalice. Anglo-Saxon influence is evident in the interweaving and biting animals. Along with the neat script this suggests that the book may have been written in Northumbria, but even so the decoration was certainly the work of an Irish illuminator. Whatever its origins, the manuscript shows that close artistic connections existed between different monasteries and the individual craftsmen within them. This working together and the cross-fertilisation that resulted was a significant factor in the creation of this 'Golden Age' for Celtic Art.

Most of the pages of the 'Book of Durrow' are bordered with interlacing bands and many of these are accentuated by the use of double lines on the edges. The darkening of spaces between these bands also gives the design greater clarity. The 'Book of Durrow' brings together the three great motifs of Celtic art – the spiral, the interlace, and the zoomorph. Strangely, only two of these are ever found on the same page, never all three.

As with the **Cathach**, open-mouthed animals are used in decoration but the bodies take on a snake-like quality. In contrast with the Cathach, the designs are much bolder in scale and complexity with clever use of rich colours. The lion symbol of the evangelist is clearly modelled on Saxon jewellery and has not yet been adapted to the Celtic idiom as happens in the great manuscripts of the following century. Other foreign features are already in process of adaptation. The idea of covering a page entirely in decoration comes from the Near East and is known as a 'carpet page'. Within the design of each carpet page is a balance and contrast between intricate detail and carefully reserved spaces for the eye to rest on.

In and around the eighth century there must have been a great number of illuminated manuscripts of which only a few managed to survive the ravages of time. Each of these has its own story to tell. The 'Book of Durrow' was for many years used a magical cure for sick cattle.

From the eighth century two great works pay testimony to the achievements of the manuscript illuminators. Both the Lindisfarne and Lichfield Gospels were made for a functional use on the altar and were preserved in metal book shrines. Small pocket Gospel books were also produced for learned men to carry throughout the continent of Europe.

Common to both Gospels is a fine use of animal interlacing, similar to that found in Germanic art but retaining an essential logic lacking in the Anglo-Saxon and Viking examples. Many designs give the impression of regularity but on closer inspection subtle irregularities can be seen. However, any discord is avoided and the balance and harmony is carefully retained. This tendency to equivalence and assymmetry continually resists classical influences throughout the seventh and eighth centuries, and would be used, later, in Celtic poetry to develop one of the most elaborate systems of metres, rhymes and assonances ever invented.

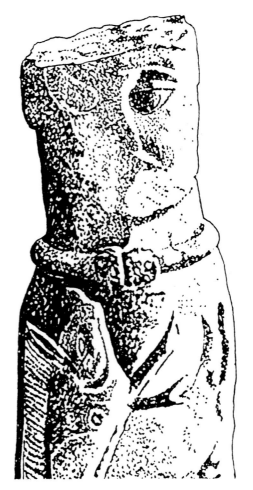

Limestone statue of a male figure with torc and boar in relief on his chest. The side of the figure is carved with a large eye,

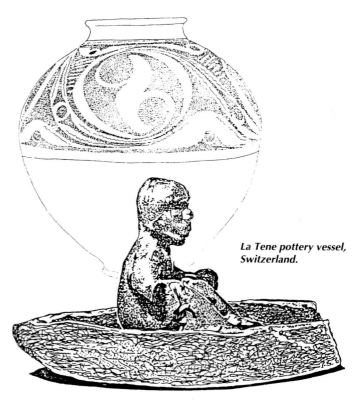

La Tene pottery vessel, Switzerland.

Votive offering of a boat with separately modelled figure of an oarsman. Clay, 10cm long. La Tene, Austria.

5. West African Ceramics

West African Ceramics

The arts of West Africa are represented in this chapter by articles from the pottery traditions of the Ashanti people from Ghana and the Hausa of Nigeria. In both cases the most important uses of pottery are as cooking vessels and water jars, although the range of forms also includes ritual objects for ceremonial occasions. In design terms the shape of the objects is closely related to the method of construction, and the decoration relates to cultural practice and traditional belief systems.

Hausa Pottery

By contrast with other parts of Africa, the greater part of Hausa pottery is made by men. Women working within family compounds do make and decorate pots but their technical methods and pottery types differ from those of men who practice a highly stylised and physically demanding beating technique, more akin to that of metal workers.

Their seemingly unlike technique enables male Hausa potters to make a range of spherical or ellipsoidal forms in clay, ranging from narrow-necked bottles to wide-mouthed cooking and storage pots. Some of these storage pots, **randa**, may be up to 600 or 700mm in diameter.

Hausa women's pottery is made by other techniques – 'flop-over' moulds, coiling, external beating – and like that of the men, it is largely for domestic use and sold in local as well as more distant markets. Women potters also make toys, dolls and other quite elaborately modelled and decorated wares.

Potmaking in Hausaland, as elsewhere in West Africa, depends on suitable locally available clay deposits and although these are widely distributed, some are recognisably better than others. The major centres of Hausa pottery production tend to be found around Sokoto, Katsina, Kano and Zaria, but minor centres may be found in all regions.

Active groups of Hausa potters have also settled elsewhere in Nigeria, especially in Nupe and in the Yoruba states south of the Niger-Benue confluence. Here they continue to practice their craft in the traditional way. As in Hausaland, many such family groups concentrate on pottery-making only during the dry season and practice subsistence farming during the rainy period.

Glazes and the potter's wheel are not used by traditional West African potters. Despite this, their wares are highly crafted, technically and functionally differentiated, and rapidly produced. Although the forms of domestic Hausa pottery derive from African rather than Islamic tradition, certain specialised wares seem likely to have been formally as well as functionally derived from Muslim prototypes

originally brought across the Saharan caravan routes from North Africa and beyond. As with West African Muslim architecture, forms were transmitted rather than techniques.

The spherical pottery water cooler, for instance, with its stirrup-handle, small-lidded filling hole and pouring spout, is fairly clearly related to similar utensils still made and used in most Mediterranean countries, but, like the Hausa handled ablution ewer, **butan salla**, it suggests a thrown form reinterpreted in hand-built terms.

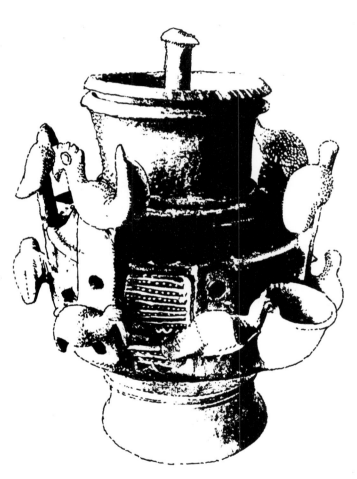

Ceremonial water jar (Tukunya)

Usually gifts to a bride are either purely decorative or serve as ornamental stands for a calabash or a basket. Some ceremonial water jugs are decorated with human and animal figures, in a circular, three-dimensional band around the pot. The significance of patterns and figures varies. These jars are made according to the inspiration of the potter, or specially commissioned, as to colouring, design and arrangement of the clay figures.

The ubiquitous Hausa inkpot, kurtan tawada, is another pottery artifact which (like the wooden writing board, allo), epitomises the pervasiveness of Muslim acculturation in Hausa society. (See page 62, item 10)

Clay and its Preparation

Local clay is dug, dried in the sun, broken into pieces, and then put into a pot of water to slake. On the following day it is turned out and mixed with grit to the required consistency. In general, no more clay is dug out at any time than sufficient to produce a day's output of pots. 'Pugging' of the body is achieved by trampling the clay on a matte surface.

The 'body' used is approximately a half and half mixture of strong sticky clay with a gritty material containing grains up to 4–5mm in diameter. For a tempering material sand is sometimes used, but for the strongest wares, a grog is made by roasting clay and pounding it to the required consistency. In granite areas (widespread throughout Hausaland) partially decomposed feldspathic gravel is used (sometimes in association with a leached tropical rock, laterite, high in iron and alumina content). Before use, this material is sieved with a mesh screen or a perforated calabash.

The quantity of tempering material or 'grog', is neither weighed nor measured. Potters judge from experience just how much to add, and are guided by the texture of the resulting clay body.

The practical advantage of pottery made from coarse 'grogged' bodies of this type and fired to low temperatures (600–650°C) lies in their resistance to thermal shock. Cooking pots made this way can be used over an open flame without breaking.

Implements (illustrated below)

1) Leaf
2) Wet rag or soft leather
3) Wooden beater or 'paddle'
4) Dry clay beater or pestle
5) Smooth stone
6) Stick with knobbed end
7) Skein of baobab seed beads
8) Twisted cord roller
9) Sharp stick

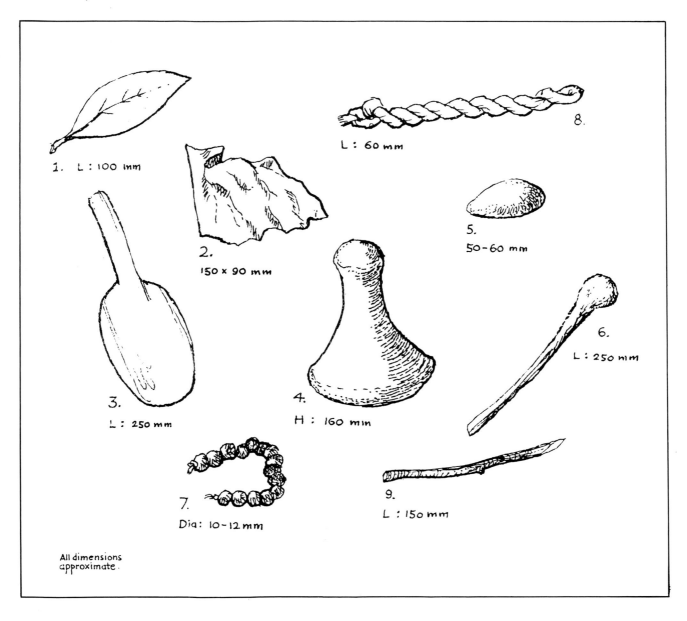

1. L : 100 mm
2. 150 × 90 mm
3. L : 250 mm
4. H : 160 mm
5. 50–60 mm
6. L : 250 mm
7. Dia : 10–12 mm
8. L : 60 mm
9. L : 150 mm

All dimensions approximate.

55

Figures 1–6

To make a spherical storage or cooking pot, the potter is seated on the ground before a small saucer-shaped depression. A ball of prepared well-grogged clay is dusted with ash or fine micaceous sand and knocked into a slightly flattened sphere in the saucer-shaped hollow. The 'opening-up' commences as the potter turns the lump with one hand while beating it rhythmically with a rounded clay beater. As the pot wall rises, it is now supported with one hand and rotated with one foot. A wooden paddle or bat-shaped beater is used alternatively with the pestle to control the rising rim and to define the form. Dusting with ash or fine sand continues intermittently. Water is used very sparingly. (This method is also used to make the almost ellipsoid water carrying pot, **tutu**. When the narrow opening will no longer accommodate hand and clay beater, a knobbed stick is introduced and used in conjunction with the wooden paddle. The neck is attached later, as described below for larger pots, when the body of the **tutu** has hardened a little).

The pot is then left to 'firm up' in a reasonably shady cool and draught-free room and when 'leather-hard' has a sausage-like roll of plastic clay 'luted' to its rim. By judicious wetting, squeezing and smoothing with his fingers and a strip of leather or a wet leaf, the potter pulls up a collar-like wall with a strong moulded edge, while he rotates the pot with his foot. So that this conjunction of plastic and leather-hard clays will not cause cracking and the later separation of pot and rim, the plastic clay is tempered with donkey dung which contains a high proportion of chaff and reduces shrinkage. Sawdust may be an acceptable substitute.

Finishing and Decorating

When thoroughly sun-baked, the pots are burnished by women. Sitting in the shade with a vessel on their left side, they have on their right a small pot containing a thin red oxided wash. Soaking a cloth in this, they paint the outside of the vessel without wetting it too much to leave a thin film of oxide on the rim and surface of the pot. Whilst still damp this is rubbed into the clay with a skein of beads, leaving the pot smooth and dully burnished. The beads are seeds from the baobab tree, bored and threaded into skeins. After firing, this polished oxide wash acquires a smooth sheen, bright red in colour. Clays containing mica respond well to this process. Alternatively, a micaceous slip may be applied to give a golden sheen, although this often occurs as a consequence of the beating technique.

1

2

3

56

Simple decoration is achieved using a wooden roller or twisted string, or with sharp sticks, to make simple geometrical designs. Some vessels are decorated with thin ropes of clay, pressed in place.

More complex decoration is applied to vessels intended for purely ornamental use. In this category are the individually commissioned painted ceremonial water pots given to brides, and painted pot stands. These are decorated with three-dimensional representations of birds and animals, colourfully painted.

Pigments used include white clay, red haematite, indigo blue, lamp black and silvery mica. Painted designs are frequently found on water coolers.

Hausa Pottery Firing

Here is a description of firing pots at the pottery of Mallam Inua, a Hausa craftsman, at the town of Bauchi:

When sufficient numbers of vessels have accumulated from each potter, a firing will be arranged. In this particular pottery an average firing includes some 35 vessels: small soup bowls, large conical pots for bathing children, different sized and shaped water containers, urns and casseroles. The potters' wives and children bring the wares near to the firing place. Careful preparation is necessary.

The same site is used time and time again. It is some 25 feet in diameter and covered with ash accumulated from previous firings. One potter has to cover the ground with a layer of dried cow dung six inches thick (brushwood is used in other localities). Meanwhile, another potter assisted by young boys brings head-load bundles of dried grass gathered from the surrounding savannah, and these are stacked nearby. A third, in the case of this particular pottery, the chief potter, undertakes the critical operation of placing the pots on the carpet of dung. Taking larger vessels first, he starts in the centre with a single pot. Working outwards, he leaves behind him a pattern of vessels resembling a huge ammonite; each conical base entered into the neck of its neighbour. On top of this pattern when completed, are placed small vessels until a rounded heap is stacked. When questioned regarding the 'ammonite' positioning, the potter merely smiled, replying "we have always done it so".

Believed by the author to be one of the many craft discoveries or developments of Nigeria, this original stacking position allows all the vessels positioned to accomplish their linear expansion constantly in an ever-widening circle; precluding crackings as the heat becomes more intense. The principle is closely analogous to expansion bends in modern engineering, and is the first of its type seen by the writer. Other traditional potteries engaged in large firing

4

5

6

Hausa potter at work in Zanu, Nigeria

merely stack their vessels, separating them one from one another with two or three potsherds, limiting the expansion of each pot to that one alone.

When the stacking is completed, faggots of dry grass are placed around the circumference of the stacked pots leaning inwards towards the top. So arranged, the grass forms a wall about two feet thick, leaving an open space still visible. This is then completely covered with layers of dried grass fuel thrown on to form a complete dome. The next operation, seemingly out of character although there is good reason for it, is to damage the crown of this heap of fuel. At a previous firing, one of the potters, with a bucketful of water, walked around the prepared covering of grass, splashing small quantities of water over it with a small calabash. On the occasion of the second firing a different potter used the same bucket and calabash, but taking large mouthfuls of water, forcibly spat them onto the grass fuel. Ejected in a large spray it was very effective and amusing. In each case both potters left about two feet up from the base undampened.

While this dampening process is taking place, the person performing the operation is followed immediately by another worker with a container of wood ash. With both hands cupped he flings this onto the dampened area, into which it both penetrates and adheres. Virtually sealing the crown when the firing takes place, it has the effect of partially clamping the pots within a more concentrated heat source, until after a while the dampened covering of fuel itself catches alight.

Ignition is done by a grass torch. Touching off one position, the potter hastens to ignite the opposite. And one cannot deny the fascination of watching the heat energy do its work while clamped by the arresting dampened covering. By the time this is also burning, the cow dung beneath has added its contribution to the firing. Finally all the fired pots rest within a heap of hot carbon and dust-ash, to cool slowly and evenly.

Stacking the pots for firing, including dampening, takes the Bauchi potters three to four hours: the actual firing lasts about half an hour. So, actually at about sunset, these modest craftsmen, leaving the sum total of three or four days production to cool overnight, depart to their huts with a murmured 'Mun gode Allah' (We thank God).

From: Jonathan Slye 'Potters of Bauchi Town, Nigeria'
Ceramic Review No. 48, Nov./Dec. 1977

FIGURE 1
A layer of accumulated ash forms a platform on which is laid a bed of small brushwood. The thoroughly sun-dried pots are laid in a circular or spiral arrangement on ground level with the mouth of one pot nestling around the base of its neighbour.

This is said to prevent cracking during firing, and certainly ensures the stability of the heap. Smaller pots are stacked on top.

FIGURE 2
When all the pots have been stacked, dried grass is placed around the circumference of the 'clamp' leaning inwards towards the top. More dried grass or discarded roof thatch is thrown on top to cover the pots and to create a conical form. (In some Hausa communities dried animal dung may be used as

an auxiliary fuel). The dome is gently beaten down to consolidate the grass. At this point the crown of the 'clamp' is dampened with water and then loosely covered with a layer of ash which serves to inhibit too rapid a temperature rise when the fire is first lit.

FIGURE 3
A blazing grass torch is applied to ignite rapidly around the base, and from opposite sides. The final temperature of 600° to 650° is not achieved until the brushwood (or dried dung) under-

lay ingnites later in the firing. The firing takes about an hour to an hour and a quarter. The pots are left overnight to cool slowly and evenly beneath the ashes.

FIGURE 4
A kind of open-topped clay-walled kiln capable of temperatures up tp 850° is extensively used by Adarawa men potters in the Sokoto area, to produce higher-fired spherical water pots, tulu. These pots combine porosity and strength and are ideal for carrying and storing water (and for keeping it cool). They are widely marketed throughout Hausaland and, despite competition from the plastic jerry-can, continue to be highly regarded.

Representational Art

New ceramic design forms have been created from the mid-twentieth century onwards. These have taken ceramic designs into new areas of architectural decoration. For example, the artist Musa Yola practiced widely in the Zaria area in the 1970s, where his painted wall decorations (often depicting his patrons) were extremely popular. Many ornamental clay wall reliefs executed by traditional builders during the 1940s and 1950s in the same area also made use of representational imagery in association with the more traditional non-figurative designs. Depictions of bicycles, motor vehicles, aeroplanes, sewing machines – all symbols of wealth and success – and the occasional human or animal figure appeared regularly in the work of popular Zaria decorators such as Mallam Ango Tukurtukur. In recent decades women's embroidery has included animal, bird and plant forms.

Mallam Jibal dan Abubaker – Section of decorated house face in Zaria, Nigeria, early 1940s

Typology

1) Flasks (**buta**)
Small, bottle-shaped, usually plain, for carrying water on journeys.

Ewers (**butan salla**)
Similar in form and general appearance to flasks, although sometimes decorated. Used for the ritual Wudu ablutions before prayer. Many regional variations exist throughout Hausaland.

2) Coolers (**kula**)
These can be either of plain red or buff clay or decorated or painted. They may have stirrup handles, spouts, stoppered mouths and ring bases. They are also found lustered, incised with geometrical designs. A twisted rope handle is occasionally seen on coolers. These vessels are porous so that when they stand in the shade and a draught, they keep the water cool.

3) Water pots (**tutu**)
These vessels are recognised by their spherical bodies and small necks. They are used by women and girls of the household to fetch water from a stream or well. Amongst the Hausa they are carried on the head. These pots frequently have burnished red bodies and a broad cream band below the neck. This band can be decorated or plain, painted, incised or stamped with a roulette pattern. The round shape and small mouth prevent spillage.

4) Cooking pots (**tukunya**)
These pots come in a variety of shapes and sizes. Uses: cooking, storing food and water. Large pots are used for boiling yams, cassava and heating water, small pots for children's food.

5) Braziers (**murfa**)
These are used widely throughout Northern Nigeria and beyond, to contain a small fire of sticks or charcoal. The basic hemispherical form is made over a flop-over mould (another pot), the foot ring added and a horseshoe-shaped opening cut out when 'leather hard'. A thick rim with three integral moulded knobs is luted to the hemispherical base. This creates a stable three point support for the cooking pot.

6) Bowls (**kasko**) *not illustrated*
These are made in a variety of deeper or shal
lower shapes for various uses – for heating or
frying, for bathing of small children, or for the
watering of animals. They have been largely
superseded by enamelled metal bowls.

7) (**kaskon suya**)
Rather like a clay cake tray, placed over the fire
to fry bean cakes in groundnut oil. Also made
moulded to a brazier.

8) Water storage jars (**randa**)
Large, usually wide-mouthed red jars standing
in the house or kitchen, into which pitchers are
poured for the daily water supply. They are
often covered with a raffia lid on which lies a
calabash dipper.

9) Painted stands (**kaskwan jere**)
Bowl-shaped vessels mounted on pedestals
used for storing small amounts of dried food,
and as stands for calabashes, baskets and other
pots. They are made by men and painted by
women. The hollow inside is used for storing
herbs, roots, etc. The number of pots mounted
on one of these stands traditionally signifies a
woman's wealth.

10) Lamps (**fitila**)
The most common form is a low-lipped bowl in
which the wick floats in groundnut oil. Others
are found in combinations of 'egg-cup' shapes,
double or multiple.

11) Inkpots (**kurtan towada**)
These are generally made by men and can be
either decorative or purely functional. Leather
or raffia thongs can be attached to them for
carrying around. They are made in various
sizes.

12) Dolls (**yar tsana**); toys (**abin wasa**)
These are often made and decorated by
women. They include clay dolls, little lidded
painted pots, toy animals and toy copies of
pitchers and bowls.

13) Moneyboxes (**gidan kudi** or **bank**)
Generally rounded, painted or lustered with
mica with a plain slit for coins. They are made
by men.

Ashanti Pottery

Potters in Ashanti are generally women, and there is a traditional taboo debarring men from practicing any aspect of this trade, from the digging of clay right through its preparation, forming, firing and even selling. Men are threatened with impotence if they take part at any stage of production. They may, however, make smoking pipes and ritualistic pottery for chiefs. These may represent anthropomorphic or zoomorphic shapes or decorative patterns.

There is a tradition that the first woman potter at the village of Taffo, an important pottery centre, was called Osra Obogyo and that she learned her art from Odomankoma, the creator. There are songs sung in her honour.

When men do make pottery they only do so where pots and pipes represent anthropomorphic or zoomorphic forms. Women are forbidden to make these. There is a story of a certain woman potter, Denta, who became barren as a result of having modelled 'figure pots'. It is also said by men that such forms are more complicated and require greater skill. A possible alternative reason why women are the chief makers of pots is that in former times pots were invariably bartered in exchange for food, and were never sold for gold dust or other currency. Thus it was not worth the time of the men to make them.

Pottery is an hereditary craft, handed down from mother to daughter. Until recent years, whole families of girls became potters, learning the art from childhood. Girls learned pottery from observation and some actual teaching. As toddlers, girls are given bits of clay to play with while their mothers and female relatives make pots. Between the ages of six and ten they begin to assist with the beating and kneading of the clay. They learn to sprinkle water on heaps of clay brought from the pits, to keep them soaked and damp for beating. As they grow older, the girls begin to make the different pots for themselves.

Younger potters do not decorate their pots with designs. Decoration is the prerogative of old and experienced potters. This is especially true in the case of 'proverb pots' and symbols used to decorate ritual vessels. 'Old' women (those past their menopause) make these. Possibly it is feared that inexperienced potters would put the wrong designs on the wrong pots, but it may also be that it is considered presumptuous for the young to make ritual pots.

In Ashanti, pottery was never confined to a particular artisan class (as is the case in Hausaland). Nearly all the women are at some time engaged in pottery, including the famous old Queen Mother of Taffo who, with her entire family, was a potter.

Under the old Ashanti regime, Taffo was one of a number of villages which were wholly engaged in making pots. Taffo pots are still exported as far as Accra, but the pottery centre has now moved to Pankronu, a short distance away from Taffo.

Pepper-grinding dish. Blackware, Ashanti

Clays used in Ashanti

Clays used in Ashanti are found along river banks. They are of several colours – white, red, yellow, grey and brown (which is less plastic and full of fine mica flakes). It is normally dug with pick-axes and hoes and carried on the head from the clay-pit to the village. The mass of clay is softened by water and pounded in mortars with pestles. It is thoroughly worked with the hands, removing large pebbles, until the required plasticity is reached. Two clays may be blended to improve quality. The kneading may be done on a board to keep the clay from contact with the ground.

Implements

1) strip of palm frond bent into a ring and used as annular scraper
2) smoothed pebbles used for polishing
3) smooth wooden 'rib' or scraper
4) dried corn from which the grains have been removed
5) piece of rag or soft leather

1.
Dia : 90 - 100 mm

Making the pots

Figure 1
A roughly spherical lump of coarsely grogged and fairly plastic clay is placed on a broad leaf (or a piece of polythene) on the ground and is hollowed out by the potter who walks slowly backwards around the pot as she begins to shape it.

Figure 2
The rim and lip are formed by drawing up the excess clay from the side walls. A piece of damp cloth dipped from time to time in water is used to refine and shape the rim.

Figure 3 and 4
The potter uses a smooth wooden 'rib' or scraper to further shape the rim and body of the pot (alternating this with the damp cloth) while she continues to walk backwards around it.

Figure 5
The neck and body of the pot are opened out and refined further with a dried corncob and then allowed to harden. The top of the pot is finished at this point and may be decorated with a wooden rim or the corncob.

Figure 6
The interior of the pot is thinned with the annular palm rib scraper (a metal version may be used).

Figure 7
The potter now finishes the outside of the base by scraping it with the corncob (the annular scraper may be used judiciously if needed). The pot is allowed to dry and may be burnished with a smooth stone at the leather-hard stage. A fine-grained red ochre slip is often used as decoration.

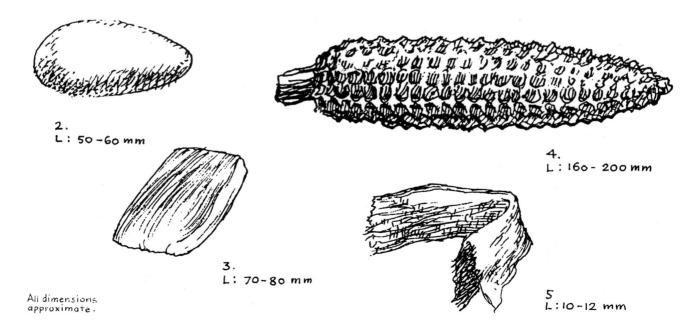

2.
L : 50 – 60 mm

3.
L : 70 – 80 mm

4.
L : 160 - 200 mm

5
L : 10 - 12 mm

All dimensions approximate.

Decorated Ware

Not all pots in Ashanti are decorated. The simplest cooking vessels and water pots are left unadorned, with the possible exception of a few incised lines or circles on the outer surface. These are generally made in the family compound and are meant for daily use.

The simplest designs are worked using sharp sticks or dried corn cobs.

Less frequently used pots, especially those intended for ceremonial use at rituals associated with birth, marriage and death, and at religious or state ceremonials, are often decorated with complex incised designs, or with carefully modelled designs of birds or animals. These are incorporated into the pots while the clay is still plastic, before sun drying.

These elaborated pots are not always made by women. Should they incorporate a human figure or head, as in the case of the 'family pots' used at funeral ceremonies, they are generally made by men. Women are forbidden to form the human figure for religious reasons, since it is believed to do so is to misuse their reproductive power, and cause sterility.

So-called 'proverb pottery' is generally made in the form of vessels, but is sometimes found in clay ornaments. These pieces are made by men or older women, past the menopause, either because of their seniority, or because of fears that younger women might make mistakes. Such pots are total designs, sometimes even the shape of the pot itself is symbolic of the proverb. It is thus very important that the correct proverb is put on the correct pot.

'Mogye Mogye' (jawbone) vessel. Blackware, Ashanti

Funerary pot

Proverb pot (typology)

Firing Ashanti Pots

Ashanti open firing methods are similar to those described for Hausa. Among the Ashanti, however, centred around Kumasi, a generously-forested area, split firewood and palm-leaf mid-ribs are a more important source of fuel than in the savannah grasslands just to the north. Outside the forest regions of Ghana, grass tends to predominate as a fuel as in Hausaland. The great variation in open firing times throughout West Africa seems to be related to the type of clay used, to the forming technique (beaten pots tending to be innately stronger) and to the availability of particular kinds of fuel.

As the temperatures achieved are invariably fairly low, the ware produced are resistant to thermal shock, enabling cooking pots to be exposed to sudden heat over an open flame without breaking.

Potters often give their wares a smooth and almost impermeable polished surface by burnishing them with smooth quartz pebbles. Besides improving the surface and reducing porosity, this increases the strength of pots by consolidation, compression and realignment of the surface particles. Much traditional Ashanti pottery is black in colour, an effect achieved after firing.

Ceremonial bowl. Blackware, Ashanti

Clay pipe bowl in form of a leopard. Ashanti.

Typology

1) Cooking pots (**esen**)

2) Soup pots (**kwasen**)

3) Water pots (**ahena**)
Used for carrying water from the stream and to store water or palm-wine in the home.

4) Water jars (**kuruwa**)}
Often ornate, used for holding drinking water.

5) Palm wine pots (**akotokyiwa**)
Used with a woven lid.

6) Braziers
Made of baked earthenware, with a hole in the top on which the cooking pot sits. Hot embers are placed in another hole in the front.

7) Pepper-grinding dish
Circular, shallow bowl, interior ribbed with concentric circles. Used for grinding roots, peppers and other vegetables for the kitchen.

8) Lamps
Various shapes, not always decorated. The simplest version is a traditional oil lamp, with a spout for one wick. A variation of this has three wicks and is also lidded. Occasionally two-tier lamps are made. All lamps are generally made in blackware.

9) Pipes (**tasen**)
Those in anthropomorphic and zoomorphic forms are always made by men. Women make simple pipe bowls decorated with geometric designs, incorporating birds, animals, fish, reptiles and even padlocks. Only the pipe bowls are made of clay, usually red-coloured and with incised detail picked out in white. The stem is of wood or corn-stalk.

10) Toys and clay ornaments
Often 'proverb pots'. Miniature water pots, used by little girls to practice carrying water on the head.

11) Pots for melting Shea butter (anane). Wheel-shaped with a hollow in the hub for melted butter.

12) Storage jars
Various sizes, used for storing dry goods. They are often unbaked, but sun-dried instead.

13) Clay bead moulds

14) Ceremonial pottery

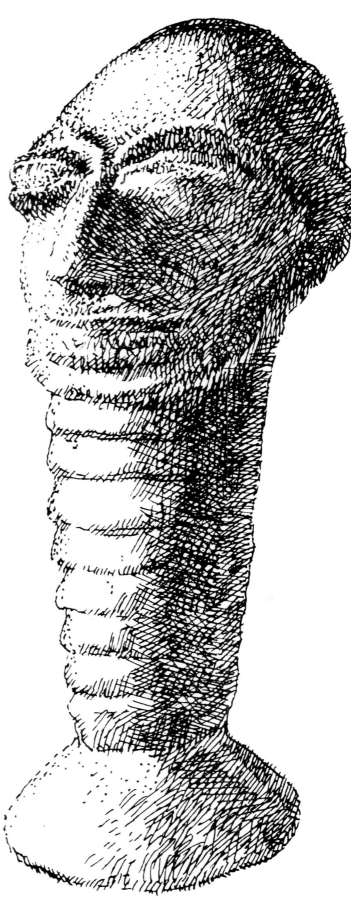

Funeral head, Ashanti.

6. Conclusion

The design traditions referred to in this book vary in cultural background and symbolic meaning. They also share some interesting and sometimes surprising similarities born from the logic of developing design systems (or 'languages') that were and are extensive in their reference to all aspects of living. New designs develop over time and often make contact with other cultures. Nevertheless, these four design traditions are but a taste of the range of systems we might have covered. The temptation to look for simple themes (body adornment, jewellery, wedding symbols) to facilitate rapid comparison across a number of cultures has been resisted in order to seek an inherent 'design sense' in the cultures presented. These four examples remain just that – examples from the wide range available through history and across continents. The intention has been to raise the possibility of similar exploration by teachers and students into areas that excite and stimulate them. The task is not as daunting as it might first appear.

A first and foremost reference source is the students' and their families' collection of objects, souvenirs and mementos. This source should not be overlooked. It is possibly the most potent starting point for any cross-cultural study. Once a theme or strand has been agreed, a second appeal to the wider local community can often rapidly amplify and develop the topic with further examples and more information. Museums and libraries can be pressed into service at this point. It is important to be clear about the focus of the project to enable museum specialists and librarians to help effectively. Their response to requests is an important aspect of the process of discovery. Many museums and libraries are vitally aware of the contextual questions that surround their collections – where did the material come from, how are the cultures presented historically and currently? Some professionals, however, may be involved in the same process of discovery as the teacher and student into how cultural material is presented, and how this presentation changes over time.

The book suggests, above all, that cross-cultural study is not a question of 'getting the correct answer' – cultural boundaries and contents are constantly shifting, particularly in response to changes in other cultures. Individuals, groups and societies, as Sarat Maharaj notes in the spirit of Collingwood's notion, based on Proudhon, that property is theft, 'beg, borrow and steal' from each other. Learning to appreciate the dynamic possibilities of cross-cultural boundary breaking is perhaps the most exciting of developments for student and teacher alike.

7. Bibliography

Islamic Design

Allgrove, J. (1976) *The Qashqa'i of Iran*
Manchester, Whitworth Art Gallery

Ardalana, N. & Bakhtiar (1973) *The Sense of Unity: The Sufi Tradition in Persian Architecture*
University of Chicago Press

Atil Esin (1975) *Art of the Arab World*
Washington DC, Smithsonian Institute

Bennett, I. (1972) *The Book of Oriental Carpets and Rugs*, London, Hamlyn

Berendson, A. (1967) *Tiles: A General History*
London, Faber

Black, D. and Loveless, C. (1979) *Woven Gardens: Nomad and Village Rugs of the Fars Province of Southern Persia*, London, David Black Oriental Carpets

Bosly, C. (1981) *Rugs to Riches: An Insider's Guide to Oriental Rugs*, London, Allen & Unwin

Brend, B. (1991) *Islamic Art*
London, British Museum Press

Burckhardt, T. (1976) *Art of Islam: Language and Meaning*, London, World of Islam Publishing Co.

Collingwood, P. (1968) *The Techniques of Rug Weaving*, London, Faber

Creswell, K. (1932) *Early Muslim Architecture*
Oxford

Diez, E. (1936) *A Stylistic Analysis of Islamic Art*
Ars Islamica III, pt. 2

Edwards, A. (1953) *The Persian Carpet: A Survey of the Carpet Weaving Industry of Persia*, Duckworth

Faegre, T. (1979) *Tents: Architecture of the Nomads*
London, John Murray

Franses, J. (1973) *Tribal Rugs from Afghanistan and Turkestan*, London, Franses of Piccadilly

Fokker, N. (1979) *Caucasian Rugs of Yesterday*
London, Allen and Unwin

Gombrich, E. (1979) *The Sense of Order: A Study in the Psychology of Decorative Art*, London, Phaidon

Grabar, O. (1964) *Islamic Architecture and its Decoration AD 800 – 1500*, London, Faber

Hill, D. & Grabar, O. (1973)
The Formation of Islamic Art, Yale University Press

Housego, J. (1978 and 1991) *Tribal Rugs*
London, Scorpion Publishing Ltd.

Hrbas, M. & Knobloch, E. (1965)
The Art of Central Asia, London, Paul Hamlyn

Hubel, R. (1964) *The Book of Carpets*
London, Barrie Jenkins

Humbert, C. (1980) *Islamic Oriental Design*
London, Faber

Islamic Carpets from the J. V. McMullen Collection
(1972) London, Hayward Gallery

Iten-Maritz, J. (1977) *Turkish Carpets*
Office du Livre

Izmidlian, G. (1977) *Oriental Rugs and Carpets Today*, Newton Abbott, Devon, David & Charles

Justin, V. (1980) *Flat Woven Rugs of the World: Kilim, Soumak and Brocading*
van Nostrand Reinholt

King, D. & Sylvester, D. (1983)
The Eastern Carpet in the Western World
London, Arts Council of Great Britain

Kybalova, L. & Darbois, D. (1969)
Carpets of the Orient, London, Hamlyn

Lane, E. (1939) *A Guide to the Collection of Tiles*
London

Lewis, B. (Ed.) (1976) paperback (1992)
The World of Islam, London, Thames & Hudson

Moynihan, E. (1979)
Paradise as a Garden in Persia and Maghul India
Aldershot, Hampshire, Scholar Press

Oz, T. (undated) *Turkish Ceramics*
Ankara, Turkish Press, Broadcasting & Tourist Dept.

Papadopoulo, A. (1980) *Islam and Muslim Art*
London, Thames & Hudson

Pope, A. (1938) *A Survey of Persian Art*
(Six Volumes), Oxford

Safadi Yasin Hamid (1978) *Islamic Calligraphy*
London, Thames & Hudson

Seher-Thoss, S. P. (1968)
Design and Colour in Islamic Architecture,
Washington DC, Smithsonian Institute

Southall, B. (1972)
Making and Decorating Pottery Tiles

Weir, S. (1976) *The Bedouin*
London, World of Islam Publishing Co.

Wilson, E. (1988) *Islamic Designs*
London, British Museum Publications

Young, G. (1978) *Return to the Marshes*
London, Futura/Macdonald & Co.

Japanese Design

Blakemore, F. (1978) *Japanese Design through Textile Patterns*, New York, Weatherhill

Blyth, R. H. (1963) *A History of Haiku* Japan, Kokuseido

Chambers, A. (1991) *Suminagaski, The Japanese Art of Marbling, London*, Thames and Hudson

Earle, J. (1980) *An Introduction to Japanese Prints* London, HMSO

Faulkner, R. *et al* (1988) *Japanese Stencils* London , Michael Joseph

Hutt, J. (1987) *Understanding Far Eastern Art* Oxford, Phaidon

Impey, O. (1981) *The Yuzen Kimono of Moriguchi Kunihiko*, Oxford, Ashmolean Museum

Japan Textile Colour Design Centre (1980) *Textile Designs of Japan*, Tokyo, Kodansha

Kodansha (1983) *Kodansha Encyclopaedia of Japan* Tokyo, Kodansha

Leach, B. and Aadachu, B. *The Living Treasure of Japan*

Lee, S. (1981) *The Genius of Japanese Design* Tokyo, Kodansha

Lowe, J. (1983) *Japanese Crafts* New York/London, Van Nostrand Reinhold

Minnich, H. (1963) *Japanese Costume and Makers of Elegant Tradition*, Tokyo, Charles E. Tuttle & Co.

Mizoguchi, S. (1973) *Design Motifs, Arts of Japan* New York, Weatherhill

Morse, E. S. (1961) *Japanese Homes and their Surroundings*, 1886, reprinted New York, Dover

Munsterberg, H. (1972) *The Folk Arts of Japan* 1958, reprinted, Tokyo, Charles E. Tuttle & Co.

Muraoka, K. and Okamura, K. (1973) *Folk Arts and Crafts of Japan*, Tokyo

Nakano, E. and Stephan B. Barbara (1982 & 1985) *Japanese Stencil Dyeing: Paste Resist Techniques* New York/Tokyo, Weatherhill

Noma, S. (1974) *Japanese Costume and Textile Arts* New York, Weatherhill

Oka, H. (1975) *How to Wrap Five More Eggs* Tokyo, Weatherhill

Picken, S. (1980) *Shinto* Tokyo, Kodansha International

Reeve, J. (Editor) (1990) *The Living Arts of Japan* London, British Museum Publication

Saburo, Enaga (1979) *Japanese Art, A Culture Appreciation*

Smith, L. and Harris, V. (1982) *Decorative Arts of the Edo Period*, London, British Museum Publications

Streeter, T. (1974 – 1989) *Kite – The Art of the Japanese Kite*, New York/Tokyo, Weatherhill

Tames, R. (1982) *The Japan Handbook (A Teacher's Guide)*, London, P. Norbury Publications

Tosenba Gallery, Joe Earle (1986) *Japanese Art and Design*, London, Victoria and Albert Museum Publications

Victoria and Albert Museum (1980) *Japan Style* London

Watson, W. (1981) *The Great Japan Exhibition* London, The Royal Academy in association with Weidenfeld and Nicholson

Yamanaka, N. (1982) *Book of Kimono* U. S., Kodansha International

Yanagi, S. (1972) *The Unknown Craftsman* Tokyo, Kodansha International

Celtic Design

Arnold, B. (1977) *A Concise History of Irish Art* London, Thames and Hudson

Bain, I. (1986) *Celtic Knotwork* London, Constable

Bain, G. (1986) *Celtic Art: The Methods of Construction*, London, Constable

Brown, P. (1980) *The Book of Kells* London, Thames and Hudson

Chadwick, N. (1985) *The Celts,* London, Pelican

Cunliffe, Barry (1975) *The Celtic World* London, Bodley Head

De Hamel, C. (1992) *Scribes and Illuminators* Medeval Craftsmen Series, London, British Museum Publications

Delaney, F. (1986) *The Celts* London, Hodder and Stoughton/BBC

Ellis Beresford, P. (1985) *Celtic Inheritance* London, Muller/Trafalgar Square

Finlay, I. (1973) *Celtic Art*, London, Faber and Faber

Forman, W. & Kruta, V. (1985) *The Celts of the West*, Los Angeles, Orbis

Green, M. J. (1989) *Dictionary of Celtic Myth and Legend*, London, Thames and Hudson

Henderson, I. (1967) *The Picts* London, Thames and Hudson

Henry, F. (1965) *Irish Art in the Early Christian Period*, London, Methuen

Jackson, K. H. (1971–6) *A Celtic Miscellany* Harmondsworth, Penguin

Kinsella, T. (Transl.) (1969) *The Tain* Oxford, Dolmen Press/Oxford University Press

Lloyd, L. (1987) *Later Celtic Art in Britain and Ireland* Shire Archaeology, Princes Risborough, Shire Publications Ltd.

Markale, J. (1978) *Women of the Celts* Gordon & Cremonesi *Celtic Civilisation*, Gordon & Cremonesi

McCana Proinsias (1970) *Celtic Mythology* Oxford, Newnes Books

Meehan, A. (1991) *Celtic Design – A Beginner's Manual*, London, Thames and Hudson

Meehan, A. (1991) *Knotwork: The Secret Method of the Scribes*, London, Thames and Hudson

Megan, R. and V. (1986) *Early Celtic Art*, Princes Risborough, Shire Archaeology, Shire Publications Ltd.

Pegg, B. (1981) *Rites and Riots: Folk Customs of Britain and Europe*, London, Blandford Press

Piggot, S. (1968) *The Druids* London, Harmondsworth

Powell, T. G. E. (1967) *The Celts* London, Thames and Hudson

Ross, A. (1970) *Everyday Life of the Pagan Celts* London, Batsford

Ryan, M. (1983) *Treasures of Ireland: Irish Art 3,000 BC – 1,500 AD*, National Museum of Ireland

Stead, I. (1985) *Celtic Art* London, British Museum Publications

Thomas, C. (1971) *Britain and Ireland in the Early Christian Period AD 400 – 800* London, Thames and Hudson

Thomas, C. (1986) *Celtic Britain* London, Thames and Hudson

West African Ceramics

Apter, D. (1963) *Ghana in Transition*
New York, Princeton University Press

Cardew, M. (1974) *View of African Pottery*
Ceramics Monthly, Feb., Vol. 22, No. 2, p. 17– 22

(1956) *Potting in Northern Nigeria*
Pottery Quarterly, Vol. 3, No. 11

(1964) *Firing the Big Pot at Kwali*
ibid, Vol. 8, No. 31, p. 63 – 65

(1979) *The Fatal Impact*
Ceramic Review 55 Jan/Feb p. 4 – 7

Clark, G. (1978) *Michael Cardew: A Portrait*
London, Faber

Carey, M. (1986) *Beads and Beadwork of East and South Africa*, Shire Ethnography, Princes Risborough, Shire Publications Ltd.

Fagg, W. & Picton, J. (1970) *The Potter's Art in Africa*, London, British Museum

Harvey, D. (1976) *Imaginative Pottery*
London, Pitman

Leigh-Ross, S. (1970) *Nigerian Pottery*, Ibadan

Levitas, B. & Morris, J. (1987) *Ornamentation, Beadwork and Clothing*, Cape Town, South Africa, College Press

Rattray, R. S. (1913) *Hausa Folklore, Customs, Proverbs* (Two Volumes) Oxford University Press

(1927) *Religion and Art in Ashanti*, Oxford University Press

Reigger, H. (1972) *Primitive Pottery*
New York and London

Smith, M. W. (Ed.) (1961) *The Artist in Tribal Society*, (Occasional paper), London, Royal Anthropological Institute

Trowell, K. M. (1960) *African Design*
London, Faber & Faber

Willett, F. (1971 and 1991) *African Art*
London, Thames and Hudson